Nita Mehta's
Vegetarian
SNACKS

Nita Mehta's
Vegetarian
SNACKS

100% TRIED & TESTED RECIPES

Nita Mehta

M.Sc. (Food & Nutrition), Gold Medalist

TANYA MEHTA

SNAB
Publishers Pvt Ltd

Nita Mehta's
Vegetarian
SNACKS

© Copyright 2003-2004 SNAB Publishers Pvt Ltd

Revised Edition 2004

ISBN 81-7869-074-8

Food Styling & Photography: SNAB

Picture on cover: Semolina Fillets
Picture on opposite: Paneer Tikka
Picture on page 2:   Instant Khaman Dhokla
Picture on page 3:   Classic Vegetarian Pizza
Picture on page 4:   Walnut Mushroom Kebabs
                         Indian Chana Pizza
Picture on page 94:   Bread Bhelpuri, Spring Dosa
Picture on back cover: Falafel, Hummus Dip

Layout and laser typesetting:

National Information Technology Academy
3A/3, Asaf Ali Road
New Delhi-110002
N.I.T.A.
☎ 23252948

Published by:

SNAB Publishers Pvt Ltd
3A/3 Asaf Ali Road
New   Delhi-110002
Tel:23250091, 23252948
Telefax:. 91-11-23250091

Editorial and Marketing office:
E-159, Greater Kailash-II, N.Delhi-110048
Tel: 91-11-29214011, 29218727, 29218574
Fax: 91-11-29225218, 29229558
E-Mail: nitamehta@email.com
         snab@snabindia.com

The Best of Cookery Books
Website: http://www.nitamehta.com
Website: http://www.snabindia.com

Printed at:
BRIJBASI ART PRESS LTD.

Distributed by:
THE VARIETY BOOK DEPOT
A.V.G. Bhavan, M 3 Con Circus
New Delhi - 110 001
Tel: 23417175, 23412567; Fax: 23415335
E-mail: varietybookdepot@rediffmail.com

Price: Rs. 195/-

Introduction

Vegetarian Snacks presents a fabulous collection of delicious recipes. Whether for a relaxed family get together or for a formal dinner party, there is a snack for every occasion. The snacks range from light and healthy to rich and filling.

The book has been organised into sections which makes it easy for you to choose your favourite snack. The various sections are - Indian party snacks, snacks from around the world, unfried and pan fried snacks, tea time snacks, innovative snacky dinners and refreshing chaats.

You may choose chatpata vegetable chaat nuggets or healthy soya balls from the Indian section, delicious pasta fritters or Japanese leafy sushi rolls from the International section, stuffed eggplant rolls and the ever popular tandoori tikkas and kebabs from the unfried and pan fried section.

The innovative Indian channa pizza where chhole bhatura's channas are poured over mango chutney kulcha and the mayo broccoli wraps are sure to be hits at high tea parties.

The snacky dinner section includes light as well as filling snacks like spring dosa which is a dosa with a Chinese stuffing and many more.

The last section of the book contains some refreshing chaats as well as chutneys to go as accompaniments with various snacks.

For the calorie conscious we have devoted a full section to pan fried and unfried snacks, reducing the oil to the minimum.

In the beginning of the book we have given a few tips which one must go through for perfect results.

Nita Mehta

Contents

Party Snacks –
From Around the World   33

Unfried & Panfried Snacks   56

Tea Time Snacks   70

Snacky Dinners 79

Refreshing Chaats 87

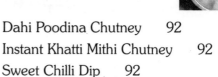

Chutneys & Dips - Indian & Oriental 91

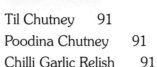

Snacky Tips

- The most delicious snack in the world can fail to tempt if it is presented in an unbecoming manner! A greasy or too oily snack is no more appetizing, so make it a habit to remove the fried snack from oil on a tissue or a paper napkin to absorb the excess oil.

- A few crisp leaves of lettuce or a sprig of mint or coriander placed at the edge of the serving platter makes the snack irresistible! Make the green leaves crisp by putting them in a bowl of cold water and keeping them in the fridge for 3-4 hours or even overnight.

- For getting a crisp coating on cutlets or rolls, dip prepared snack in a thin batter of maida & water & then roll in bread crumbs. Fry till well browned.

- In the absence of bread crumbs, a mixture of ¼ cup maida and ½ cup suji may be used to get a crisp coating.

- You may add some seasoning to the coating mixture. Finely chopped coriander or parsley or roughly crushed peppercorns or sesame seeds (til) or poppy seeds (khus-khus) etc. when added to bread crumbs give a different look to the snack. Remember to add a pinch of salt too. Sometimes a little tandoori red colour or haldi added to the coating mix gives a nice colour to the snack instead of the usual brown.

- If your cutlets fall apart, quickly tear 1-2 slices of bread and grind in a mixer to get fresh bread crumbs. Add it to the cutlet mixture for binding.

- To make crisp potato chips, soak them in cold water for 1 hour. Drain. Wipe dry and sprinkle some maida (plain flour) on them before frying.

- Never start frying in smoking hot oil as it will turn the snack black. Never fry in cold oil also as the snack may fall apart or it may soak a lot of oil.

- For deep frying any snack, add small quantities to the oil at one time. This maintains the oil's temperature. If too many pieces are added together, the oil turns cold and a lot of oil is then absorbed by the snack.

- After deep frying, let the oil cool down. Add a little quantity of fresh oil to the used oil before reusing. This prevents the oil from discolouring.

Party Snacks - INDIAN

Moong Paneer Shooters

The moong dal coating imparts a special flavour to these shooters.

Serves 4

125 gms paneer- cut into ¾" squares of ½" thickness, 1 capsicum- cut into 1" pieces
1 tomato - cut into 4 pieces lengthwise, pulp removed and cut into 1" pieces
some chat masala

BATTER
1 cup dhuli moong dal (dehusked moong beans) - soaked for 1-2 hours
2 tbsp fresh coriander - chopped very finely, 1 green chilli - chopped very finely
¾ tsp salt, ½ tsp red chilli powder or less, as desired
1-2 pinches of tandoori red colour

1. Soak dal for 1-2 hours. Strain. Grind in a mixer without water to a smooth thick paste. Put in a bowl. Beat well with hands to make it light.
2. Add coriander, green chilli, salt and chilli powder to dal paste. Add enough colour to get a bright orange colour. Keep aside.
3. Sprinkle chat masala on the paneer, capsicum and tomato nicely. Mix lightly.
4. Thread a capsicum (wrong side facing you), then a paneer and then a tomato piece (right side facing you) on each tooth pick. Keep aside till serving time.
5. To serve, heat oil for deep frying. Dip the paneer sticks in the prepared dal batter. Coat well with the fingers, sticking the batter nicely.
6. Deep fry till golden. Serve hot sprinkled with some chat masala.

Vegetable Chaat Nuggets

Delicious and soft nuggets with a crisp covering, similar in taste to the pao bhaji mixture.

Serves 4

1 cup chopped cabbage
1 cup chopped cauliflower (tiny florets)
½ cup shelled peas
2 potatoes - boiled and grated
½ cup very finely chopped carrots
3 tbsp oil
1 tsp ginger-garlic paste
2½ tsp pao-bhaji masala
2 bread slices- churned in a mixer to get fresh crumbs
¾ tsp salt, or to taste, ½ tsp sugar
1 tsp chat masala
1 tbsp lemon juice

COATING
½ cup suji, ¼ cup maida
½ tsp salt, ½ tsp pepper

1. Pressure cook cabbage, cauliflower and peas with ½ cup water to give 2 whistles. Reduce heat and keep on low heat for 3-4 minutes. Remove from fire and let the pressure drop. After the pressure drops, mash the vegetables. If there is any extra water present, dry it on fire.

2. Heat oil. Add ginger-garlic paste. Stir. Add pao-bhaji masala. Stir for a minute.

3. Add pressure cooked and mashed vegetables. Saute for 2-3 minutes.

4. Add potatoes and cook, stirring for 3-4 minutes.

5. Add chopped carrots. Add salt, sugar, chat masala and lemon juice. Mix well for 2-3 minutes. Remove from fire and let the mixture cool down.

6. Shape into balls. Flatten to get oval, flat tikkis.

7. For the coating, mix suji, maida, salt and pepper and spread on a plate.

8. Roll the tikkis over the maida- suji mixture to coat well. Refrigerate for 2 hours to get crisp nuggets.

9. At serving time, deep fry 1-2 pieces at a time in medium hot oil till crisp. Remove on paper napkins. Sprinkle some chat masala and serve hot.

Matar Makhana Kebabs

Delicious crunchy green kebabs. Very appetizing to look at!

Makes 8 kebabs

1 cup boiled or frozen shelled peas
1 cup makhanas (puffed lotus seeds)
1 tbsp oil
2 green chillies - chopped
2-3 tbsp cashewnuts (kaju)
¾ tsp salt or to taste
½ tsp pepper
¼ tsp garam masala
seeds of 4-5 chhoti illaichi (green cardamoms) - crushed

1. Heat 1 tbsp oil in kadhai. Add makhanas and saute for 3-4 minutes.
2. Add kaju and saute till kaju starts changing colour. Remove them from kadhai.
3. In the same kadhai (without any oil leftover), add peas and saute for 2 minutes. Remove peas from kadhai.
4. Grind makhanas and kaju together to a rough powder.
5. Grind peas with green chillies to a fine green paste.
6. Mix makhanas and green pea paste. Add salt, pepper, garam masala and chhoti illaichi.
7. Makes small balls and flatten them to get small round kebabs (tikkis).
8. Shallow fry on a hot tawa or pan in 1-2 tbsp oil till brown & crisp on both sides.
9. Sprinkle chaat masala and serve hot with dahi poodina chutney given on page 92.

Paneer Kolhapuri

Fragrant batter fried paneer cubes. Must give it a try.

Serves 3-4

200 gms paneer - cut into 8 big pieces

GRIND TOGETHER TO A PASTE
½" piece ginger, 2-3 flakes garlic
2 saboot kali mirch (peppercorns), 2 laung (cloves)
seeds of 2 chhoti illaichi (green cardamoms)
1 tsp jeera (cumin seeds), 2 tsp saboot dhania (coriander seeds)
¾" stick dalchini (cinnamon)
¾ tsp saunf (fennel)
½ tsp red chilli powder, ½ tsp salt

COATING
4 tbsp besan (gramflour)
2 tbsp thick curd
1 tbsp chopped fresh dhania
2 tsp kasoori methi (dry fenugreek leaves)
¼ tsp salt, ¼ tsp red chilli powder
¼ tsp ajwain (carom seeds)

1. Grind together ginger, garlic along with all the other ingredients to a fine paste. Use a little water if required.
2. Mix the ground paste with the paneer and cover with plastic wrap. Keep aside in the refrigerator till the time of serving.
3. At the time of serving, heat oil in a kadhai.
4. Sprinkle the coating ingredients on the paneer and mix well to coat. Add more besan if the paste does not stick to the paneer nicely.
5. Deep fry 2-3 pieces at a time till golden.
6. Serve hot with poodina chutney given on page 91, onion rings and lemon wedges.

Final Recipe

15

Special Shami Kebab

Serves 4

½ cup kale chaane (black gram)
1 tbsp chaane ki dal (split Bengal gram)
1-2 laung (cloves), 1-2 saboot kali mirch (peppercorns)
½" piece ginger - chopped, 1 dry red chilli, 2 tbsp cornflour
salt to taste, ¼ tsp amchoor (dried mango powder)

FILLING
1 tbsp chopped mint (poodina), 3-4 tbsp grated mozzarella cheese, 2 pinches salt

1. Soak kale chaane with chaane ki dal overnight or for 6-8 hours in 2 cups of water.
2. Pressure cook kale chaane, chaane ki dal, laung, saboot kali mirch, ginger and red chilli together. After the first whistle, keep on slow fire for 20 minutes.
3. If there is extra water, dry the chaanas for sometime on fire. There should just be a little water, enough to grind the channas to a fine paste.
4. Grind to a fine paste. Add cornflour, salt and amchoor to taste.
5. Mix all ingredients of the filling together.
6. Make a small ball of the paste. Flatten it, put 1 tsp of filling and make a ball again. Flatten it slightly.
7. Shallow fry 4-5 pieces on a tawa in 3-4 tbsp oil on medium flame. Serve with poodina chutney.

Cheesy Til Crispies

Serves 4

4 bread slices - remove sides , 4- 6 tsp til (sesame seeds)

MIX TOGETHER
3 medium potatoes - boiled and mashed
½ cup maida (plain flour)
1 tbsp chopped coriander, 1 green chilli- chopped finely
2 cubes grated cheese
¼ tsp baking powder, salt & pepper to taste

1. Except til & bread, mix all the above ingredients with potatoes. Check seasoning.
2. Cut each bread slice into 4 squares or cut in any shape (round, triangle etc).
3. Spread 1 tbsp of the potato mixture on each piece.
4. Sprinkle some til on each piece and press lightly with fingers, so that it sticks.
5. Deep fry in hot oil with the til side first in oil. Fry till potatoes turn light brown & til seeds show nicely. Drain on paper. Serve hot with tomato sauce or chutney.

Dakshini Squares

A really low calorie snack with a South Indian touch.

Serves 4   *Picture on page 67*

75 gm paneer - crumbled (¾ cup), 2 tbsp suji (semolina)
½ tsp salt, or to taste, ¼ tsp pepper, or to taste
½ onion - very finely chopped, 2 tbsp curry leaves
½ tomato - cut into half, deseeded and chopped finely
3 bread slices - toasted in a toaster
½ tsp rai (small brown mustard seeds)
3 tsp oil to shallow fry

1. Mix the suji, salt and pepper with the paneer using your fingers.
2. Add the onion, tomato and curry leaves.
3. Spread paneer mixture carefully on toasted bread slices, keeping edges neat.
4. Sprinkle some rai over the paneer mixture, pressing down gently with finger tips.
5. Heat 1 tsp oil in a non stick pan. Add a slice of bread with topping side down.
6. Cook until the topping turns golden brown and crisp. Add a little more oil for the next slice if required. Cut each slice into 4 pieces and serve hot.

Note: This recipe will work best using a minimum quantity of oil for frying.

Soya Balls

A nutritive and delicious snack, a hit both with the adults as well as the children. Do try it!

Makes 15

1 cup soya granules (nutri nugget granules)
100 gms paneer - grated (1 cup)
2 bread slices - torn in pieces and churned in a mixer to get fresh bread crumbs
1 tsp garam masala, 1 tsp salt, ½ tsp red chilli powder
1½ tbsp tomato ketchup
2 tbsp green coriander - chopped, 1 green chilli - finely chopped

1. Soak soya granules in 1 cup of hot water for 15 minutes.
2. Strain. Squeeze out the water well from the soya granules. (No water should remain).
3. Mix paneer, fresh bread crumbs, garam masala, salt, red chilli powder, tomato ketchup, chopped green coriander, green chilli and the soya granules. Mix well.
4. Make small round balls out of the soya mixture.
5. Heat oil in a kadhai and deep fry the balls on medium heat till crisp and golden. Serve hot with tomato sauce or chilli garlic relish as given on page 91.

Cocktail Corn Fritters

Fritters are batter fried dumplings, resembling pakoras.

Picture on page 68   *Serves 6- 8*

3 large soft bhuttas or fresh corns (corn on cobs)
1¼ tbsp besan (gram flour)
2 tbsp chopped green coriander
1 green chilli - chopped
1 tsp salt or to taste
¼ tsp pepper
oil for frying
lettuce leaves - for garnishing

MIXED CHUTNEY TO SERVE
¼ cup khatti mithi chutney (see page 92)
¼ cup poodina chutney (see page 91)

1. Grate the corn on the cobs (bhutta).
2. Add besan, coriander and chopped green chilli to the grated corn. Mix well. Keep aside.
3. At serving time, add salt and pepper. Mix well. Heat oil for frying. Drop 1 tbsp of batter in medium hot oil, with the help of a spoon. (See picture given on the side).
4. Fry 4-5 pieces at a time till golden brown on both sides.
5. Drain on a paper napkin.
6. Mix both the chutneys to get a spicy sauce. Pour the sauce in a small bowl.
7. Line the plate with fresh lettuce leaves and place the hot corn fritters on it.
8. Dot each fritter with the prepared chutney. Serve hot.

Drop 1 tbsp of batter in medium hot oil with the help of spoon.

Hare Bhare Kebabs

Serves 8

1 cup channe ki dal (split gram)
1 bundle (600 gm) spinach - discard stalks and keep only leaves, chop leaves finely
3 tbsp oil
3 slices bread- churned in a mixer to get fresh bread crumbs
2 tbsp cornflour
2 green chillies - chopped finely
½ tsp red chilli powder, ½ tsp garam masala
¾ tsp salt or to taste, ½ tsp amchoor (dried mango powder)

SPICES - CRUSH TOGETHER
½ tsp jeera (cumin seeds), seeds of 2 moti illaichi (black cardmom)
3- 4 saboot kali mirch (black peppercorns), 2- 3 laung (cloves)

FILLING
½ cup grated paneer, 2 tbsp chopped coriander
salt and bhuna jeera (roasted cumin seeds) powder to taste

1. Crush jeera, seeds of moti illaichi, kali mirch and laung together.
2. Clean, wash dal. Pressure cook dal with the above crushed spices, ½ tsp salt and 2 cups water. After the first whistle, keep the cooker on slow fire for 15 minutes. Remove from fire and keep aside.
3. After the pressure drops down, mash the hot dal with a karchhi. If there is any water, mash the dal on fire and dry the dal as well while you are mashing it. Remove from fire. Remove to a large mixing bowl.
4. Discard stem of spinach and chop leaves very finely. Wash in several changes of water. Leave the chopped spinach in the strainer for 15 minutes so that the water drains out. Heat oil in a kadhai and saute spinach leaves for 8-10 minutes till absolutely dry and well fried. Remove from fire.
5. Tear 3 slices of bread into pieces and churn in a mixer to get fresh bread crumbs.
6. Add fresh bread crumbs, cornflour, spinach, green chillies, salt and masalas to the mashed dal. Make small balls. Keep aside.
7. For the filling, mix paneer, coriander, salt and jeera. Flatten spinach-dal balls and put 1 tsp paneer filling. Cover the filling and form a flattened tikki.
8. Cook them on a tawa with just 4 tbsp oil till brown on both sides. When done shift them on the sides of the tawa so that they turn crisp and the oil drains out while more kebabs can be added to the hot oil in the center of the tawa. Remove the kebabs on paper napkins and serve hot with hari chutney.

Badaami Aloo

Picture on facing page   *Serves 6*

3 big (longish) potatoes
1 tbsp melted butter, some chaat masala to sprinkle

FILLING
3 almonds - crushed with a belan (rolling pin)
4 tbsp grated paneer (50 gm)
1 tbsp poodina (mint) leaves - chopped, 1 green chilli - deseeded and chopped
¼ tsp garam masala, ¼ tsp red chilli powder, ¼ tsp salt, a pinch amchoor

COVERING
½ cup thick curd - hang in a muslin cloth for 30 minutes, 1 tbsp ginger paste
¼ tsp red chilli powder, ¾ tsp salt, ¼ tsp orange tandoori colour or haldi

CRUSH TOGETHER TO A ROUGH POWDER
2-3 blades of javitri (mace)
1 tsp shah jeera (black cumin), seeds of 2 moti illaichi (brown cardamom)
6-8 saboot kali mirch (peppercorns)

1. Boil potatoes in salted water till just tender. When they are no longer hot, peel skin.
2. Mix all the ingredients written under filling in a bowl.
3. Grind or crush shah jeera, seeds of moti illaichi, peppercorns, and 2-3 pinches of javitri to a coarse powder.
4. To the paneer mixture, add ¼-½ teaspoon of the above freshly ground spice powder also. Keep the leftover powder aside.
5. Mix hung curd, ginger paste, the left over freshly ground powder and red chilli powder and salt. Add haldi or orange colour.
6. Run the tip of a fork on the surface of the potatoes, making the surface rough. (The rough surface holds the masalas well).
7. Cut each potato into 2 halves, vertically. Scoop out, just a little, to get a small cavity in each potato with the back of a teaspoon. Rub some melted butter on the inside and outside surface of the potatoes. Stuff with paneer filling.
8. With a spoon apply the curd mixture on the outside (backside) of the potatoes and on the rim also (not on the filling).
9. Grill potatoes in a gas tandoor or a preheated oven at 210°C/410°F for 15 minutes on a greased wire rack till they get slightly dry.
10. Spoon some oil or melted butter on them (baste) and grill further for 10 minutes till the coating turns dry. Sprinkle some chaat masala and serve hot.

Vegetarian Seekhs : Recipe on page 62 ➢

Stuffed Eggplant Rolls

A foreign recipe made local by creating an Indian filling for the roll. A cold snack, ideal as a light starter for a summer meal.

Serves 4   *Picture on Opposite page*

1 big eggplant (bharte waala baingan) - cut lengthwise into thin (1/8" thick) slices
few tooth picks, 1 tbsp oil

FILLING
1 cup boiled or frozen peas - grind to a rough paste
2 tbsp oil, ½ tsp jeera (cumin seeds)
1 onion - finely chopped, 1 tsp finely chopped ginger
½ tsp garam masala, ¼ tsp red chilli powder, ½ tsp salt

1. Sprinkle salt on eggplant slices. Let it sit for 15 minutes to sweat. Rinse and pat dry.
2. For filling, heat 2 tbsp oil. Add jeera. Wait for a minute.
3. Add onion and ginger. Cook till onions turn soft. Add paste of peas, salt, garam masala and red chilli powder. Keep filling aside.
4. Put 1 tbsp oil in a nonstick pan. Swirl the pan to coat the base of pan with oil.
5. Place eggplant slices and pan fry both side till brown patches appears on both the sides.
6. Place 1 tbsp filling on the edge of a slice and roll. Fasten the edge with tooth pick and serve at room temperature.

◁ *Oat Fudge Fingers : Recipe on page 77*

Paneer Tikka

Picture on page 1   *Serves 4*

**300 gm paneer - cut into 1½" pieces of 1" thickness
1 large capsicum - deseeded and cut into 1" pieces (12 pieces)
1 onion - cut into 4 pieces and then separated**

**MARINADE
½ cup dahi- hang in a muslin cloth for 15 minutes
3 tbsp thick malai or thick cream**

**GRIND TOGETHER
1" piece ginger, 5-6 flakes garlic
2 dried, whole red chillies - soak in 3 tbsp water for 10 minutes and drain
a few drops of orange colour or a pinch of haldi (turmeric)
1½ tbsp oil, 1 tbsp (level) cornflour
½ tsp amchoor, ¾ tsp salt, or to taste, ½ tsp chaat masala
1 tbsp tandoori masala or ½ tsp garam masala**

1. Hang curd in a muslin cloth (mal-mal ka kapda) for 15 minutes.
2. Transfer the hung curd to a flat bowl. Beat till smooth.
3. Soak red chillies in some water. Drain through a sieve (channi)
4. Grind ginger, garlic, soaked red chillies, 1½ tbsp oil, cornflour, amchoor, salt, kala namak, tandoori masala and colour or haldi to a smooth paste in a mixer.
5. Add the paste to the hung curd in the flat bowl. Add cream or malai.
6. Add paneer to the paste. Mix well so that all pieces of paneer get well coated with the marinade on all the sides.
7. Grease the wire rack of the oven well with oil. Arrange paneer on the greased rack. After arranging all the paneer pieces on the wire rack, put the capsicum and onions - both together in the left over marinade in which paneer was kept. Mix well to coat the vegetables with the marinade. Leave the vegetables in the bowl itself.
8. About 1 hour before serving, put the paneer pieces placed on the wire rack in the hot oven at about 200°C. Grill for 15 minutes or till almost done. Grill the paneer till it gets slightly dry. Switch off the oven and let them be in the oven till serving time.
9. At serving time, brush the pieces with 2 tbsp of melted butter or sprinkle some oil on the paneer pieces (basting). Now remove the vegetables from the bowl and put them also in the oven on the sides of the paneer. Grill everything together for another 10 minutes. The vegetables should not be grilled for too long.
10. Remove from the oven. Serve immediately (really hot), sprinkled with some lemon juice and chaat masala with dahi poodina chutney given on page 92.

Walnut Mushroom Kebabs

Serves 6- 8   *Picture on page 4*

200 gm mushrooms - chopped finely
2 potatoes - boiled and grated
1 big onion - chopped finely
½ cup boiled peas
4 green chillies - chopped, 1" piece ginger - chopped very finely
2 tbsp chopped coriander
1 tsp garam masala powder
½ tsp amchoor
½ tsp red chilli powder, 1½ tsp salt, or to taste
2 bread slices- torn into pieces and churned in a mixer to get fresh bread crumbs

TOPPING
¼ cup grated mozzarella cheese or pizza cheese (25 gm)
2 tbsp akhrot (walnuts) - crushed coarsely on a chakla belan

1. Heat 3 tbsp oil. Add chillies, ginger and onion. Cook till onions turn transparent.
2. Add mushrooms. Stir for 4-5 minutes, till they turn dry. Remove from fire (see picture).

3. Add all the other ingredients. Check the spices & salt.
4. Shape into small flattened circles or rounds.
5. Heat 1 tsp oil in a non-stick pan. Saute 3- 4 kebabs till golden brown on both sides.
6. When the circles are done, remove from fire. Grate ½ tsp cheese and sprinkle some crushed walnuts on each circle. Spread it in the centre of the circle, leaving the edges (see picture given on the side).

7. In a microwave place the topped kebabs with the cheese side up. Microwave for 1-2 minutes or till cheese melts. Serve hot with chilli garlic chutney.

Note: If you do not have a microwave then place the topped kebabs with the cheese side up in a non stick pan and cook covered on low heat for 1-2 minutes or till cheese melts.

Grate ½ tsp cheese on each piece.

Nutty Sago Puffs

Serves 6

½ cup saboodana - soaked in 1 cup warm water for 1 hour
2 tsp khus khus (poppy seeds), 3 potatoes - boiled and grated
2 slices bread - tear into pieces and grind in a mixer to get fresh crumbs
1 tsp chopped ginger, 1 green chilli- chopped
2 tbsp chopped green coriander
½ tsp garam masala, ½ tsp red chilli powder, ½ tsp amchoor, 1 tsp salt
½ cup roughly mashed paneer
1 tbsp thick malai
12 kishmish - soaked in water

1. Soak saboodana in about 1 cup warm water to cover it for ½-1 hour or till soft. Drain off excess water by keeping in a strainer.
2. Mix boiled potatoes, fresh bread crumbs, green chilli, ginger, coriander, garam masala, red chilli powder, amchoor, salt and khus- khus. Lastly mix in the paneer gently. Shape into 12 balls. Flatten each ball and place a drop of malai and 1 kishmish. Make a ball again and flatten to get oval pieces.
3. Press each piece on saboodana spread on a plate so that it sticks. Flatten some more. Deep fry 2-3 pieces in a kadhai at a time in medium hot oil till golden.

Khus Poha Tikkis

Makes 12- 14

2 cups poha (pressed rice) - soaked in water for 15 minutes
1 tsp very finely chopped ginger, 1 tbsp lemon juice
1 green chilli - chopped, 2 tbsp chopped curry leaves or coriander
½ tsp garam masala, 1 tsp salt, or to taste
¼ cup khus khus (poppy seeds)
4 tbsp oil for frying

1. Wash poha well and soak it in 2 cups of water for 15 minutes.
2. Drain & squeeze well (press in between your palms, no water should remain).
3. Add salt, garam masala, ginger, lemon juice, green chilli and curry leaves or green coriander. Mix well.
4. Make small tikkis, about 2" in diameter. Roll over khus khus scattered on a plate.
5. Heat oil in a pan and fry on a medium heat till crisp and golden brown.
6. Serve hot with poodina chutney.

Hara Channa Kebab

Fresh green gram has been used to churn out deliciously succulent kebabs.

Makes 14

2 cups fresh green gram (hara channa or chholia)
½ cup besan (gramflour) - roasted on a tawa for 1 minute, or till fragrant
2 slices bread - torn into pieces and churned in a mixer to get fresh crumbs
1 cup yogurt- hang in a muslin cloth for 30 minutes
3 tbsp oil
1 tsp jeera (cumin seeds)
1 small onion - chopped
1 tbsp ginger-garlic paste
3- 4 green chillies - chopped
10- 12 fresh curry leaves
1 tbsp tandoori masala
1 tsp salt or to taste
2-3 tbsp maida (plain flour)

CRUSH TOGETHER
1 tbsp saboot dhania (coriander seeds)
1 tsp jeera - roasted on a tawa (bhuna jeera)
½ tsp saboot kali mirch (black peppercorns)

1. Crush saboot dhania, bhuna jeera and saboot kali mirch on a chakla-belan (rolling board-pin).
2. Clean, wash hara chholia. Pressure cook hara chhole with the above crushed spices, ½ tsp salt and 1 cup water. Give one whistle. Remove from fire and keep aside. After the pressure drops down, mash the hot hara chholia with a potato masher or a karchhi. If there is any water, mash and dry the chholia on fire. Remove from fire.
3. Heat 3 tbsp oil, add jeera, let it change colour. Add chopped onion, ginger-garlic paste, chopped green chillies and curry leaves. Cook till onions turn light brown.
4. Add mashed chholia, salt, roasted besan, tandoori masala and hung yogurt. Cook for 5 minutes or till dry. Remove from fire. Cool.
5. Add bread crumbs and mix well.
6. Make marble sized balls of the chholia mixture. Flatten to form a kebab of about 2" diameter. Roll in maida and keep in the fridge till serving time.
7. At the time of serving, shallow fry 3-4 pieces at a time on a hot tawa in 6 tbsp oil. Turn sides till both sides are crisp. Remove the kebabs on paper napkins. Serve.

Kebab-e-Dil

Heart shaped delicious vegetable cakes

Makes 8-10 pieces

½ cup suji (semolina)
1 cup milk
1 tbsp butter
1 cup finely diced mixed vegetables (4-6 beans, 1 carrot, ¼ cup finely chopped cabbage)
½ cup roughly mashed paneer
2 slices bread - grind in a mixer to get fresh bread crumbs
¼ cup coriander leaves - chopped
2 green chillies - chopped finely
salt to taste
¼ tsp garam masala
½ tsp red chilli flakes or powder
½ tsp chaat masala
2 tsp lemon juice
1 tsp tomato sauce

1. Heat butter in a kadhai. Add very finely chopped carrots and beans and ¼ tsp salt. Saute for 2 minutes. Cook covered on low heat for 2 minutes till crisp-tender. Add cabbage and stir for 2 minutes. Remove vegetables from kadhai and keep aside.
2. To the same kadhai, add suji and stir fry on low heat for just 2-3 minutes.
3. Add milk, stirring continuously. Cook till thick. Keep on low flame for 1-2 minutes more, stirring constantly, until dry and forms a lump.
4. Add paneer and coriander. Mix well.
5. Remove from fire. Transfer to a paraat or a big mixing bowl. Add vegetables and all other ingredients. Mix very well. Check seasonings. Make heart shaped tikkis with greased or wet hands.
6. Shallow fry 4-5 pieces at a time in a pan in 3-4 tbsp oil till done. Serve with hari chutney.

Note: To make crisper tikkis keep them in the fridge, for 15-20 minutes before frying, to set them well.

Semolina Fillets

*This is called fillet, because inspite of being a vegetarian snack it tastes like fish.
So, enjoy the taste of fish in a vegetarian version.*

Serves 6   *Picture on cover*

1 cup suji (semolina)
1½ cups milk, ¼ cup oil
50 gm paneer- grated (½ cup)
1½ tsp salt, ½ tsp red chilli powder, ½ tsp garam masala
1 tbsp chopped coriander
a pinch of nutmeg (jaiphal) - powdered

FRYING
2 tbsp cornflour mixed with ¼ cup water to make a very thin batter
**1½ cup cornflakes - crushed coarsely on a chakla belan or 2 bread slices - torn into
pieces and churned in a mixer to get fresh bread crumbs**

1. Heat oil and milk in a kadhai.
2. Sprinkle suji gradually, stirring with the other hand till well mixed. Cook on low heat, stirring continuously till it turns dry and the grains become clear. Cook further till it forms into a lump.
3. Remove from fire and add paneer, masalas, coriander. and jaiphal powder or some grated jaiphal.
4. Put the mixture on the back side of a wet plate and make a block of a square shape of about ½" thickness or slightly less, with help of a knife (see picture given below). Let it cool down. Keep in the fridge for ½ hour.
5. Cut the mixture in diamond shape (see below) or cut it in square shape.
6. Pick up each piece carefully and dip in the cornflour paste. Press over crushed cornflakes or bread crumbs scattered on a plate. Coat well to cover all the sides. Deep fry 2-3 at a time to a golden colour. Serve hot.

*Give it a neat square shape
with help of knife or hands.*   *Cut mixture into diamond shaped pieces.*

Hariyaali Idlis

Delicious green-paalak idlis. Tastes good even without sambhar & chutney.

Serves 8

1 packet (200 gm) ready-made idli mix
1½ cups chopped spinach
2- 3 green chillies - deseeded & chopped
½ tsp eno fruit salt
a few cashewnuts or blanched almonds - split into two halves, optional

TOPPING
2 cups fresh curd - beat well till smooth
½ tsp salt

TEMPERING (TADKA)
2 tbsp oil
1 tsp rai (small brown mustard seeds)
½ tsp jeera (cumin seeds)
2 green chillies - chopped
1 small tomato - chopped finely
2- 3 tbsp curry leaves

1. Mix the idli mix according to the instructions on the packet.
2. Grind the chopped spinach and green chillies in a mixer to a smooth paste with 1-2 tbsp water.
3. Add the spinach paste to the idli mixture. Add ¼ tsp salt & ½ tsp eno fruit salt. Mix well.
4. Grease a mini idli mould. Put a little batter in each cup and top with a split cashewnut or almond on each idli. Steam for 14-15 minutes on medium flame till a knife inserted in the idli comes out clean. If a mini mould is not available, make small flat idlis by putting a little less batter in the normal idli mould.
5. Place the steamed idlis in a large bowl.
6. Beat the curd with salt till smooth. Pour the curd over the idlis in the bowl. Mix gently. Keep aside for 10-15 minutes.
7. Transfer the idlis to a flat serving platter or a shallow dish. Keep aside till serving time.
8. To serve, heat 2 tbsp oil. Add rai and jeera. When they stop spluttering, add green chillies, tomato and curry leaves. Stir to mix all ingredients and immediately pour over the idlis covered with curd.
9. Serve immediately.

Paneer Makai Tikri

Makes 10-12

200 gm paneer - crumbled
oil to shallow fry

MIX TOGETHER
2 potatoes - boiled and mashed
½ cup tinned or fresh boiled corn (see note)
3 slices bread - broken into pieces and crumbled in a mixer to get fresh crumbs
½ tsp garam masala
½ tsp black pepper powder
1½ salt, or to taste
½ tsp red chilli powder
½ tsp amchoor powder
2 pinches of haldi
2 tbsp poodina (mint) - finely chopped
1 tbsp very finely chopped ginger
1 green chilli - deseeded and chopped finely

1. Mix all ingredients with the mashed potatoes.
2. Mix paneer into the mixture lightly.
3. Divide the mixture into equal portions. Shape each portion into a ball.
4. Flatten the balls into tikkis, smoothening the edges.
5. Shallow fry 2-3 pieces at a time in 2-3 tbsp oil on a tawa or a nonstick pan. When these are done, shift the tikkis to the sides of the tawa and let them be there on low heat for a while, so that they turn crisp. Add a tbsp oil in the centre and fry another batch in the meantime. Drain on absorbent paper.
6. Serve hot with chutney.

Note: To boil fresh corn, put 4- 5 skinned whole corns in a pressure cooker. Add 2 tsp salt, 2 tsp sugar and a pinch of haldi. Add enough water to cover the corns. Pressure cook to give 1 whistle and then keep on low heat for 5 minutes. After the pressure drops, remove the corn kernels. These can be stored in an air tight box in the freezer compartment of the refrigerator for a month or even more.

Hyderabadi Rolls

Serves 8

2 potatoes - chopped
¾ of a small cauliflower - cut into small florets
2 onions - chopped
1 cup boiled or frozen shelled peas
4 slices of bread - broken into pieces and ground in a mixer to get fresh crumbs
1" piece ginger and 5-6 flakes garlic - ground to a paste (2 tsp)
½ tsp red chilli powder, ½ tsp garam masala, 1½ tsp salt or to taste
2 tsp tomato sauce
1 green chilli - finely chopped, 2 tbsp chopped fresh poodina
4-5 tbsp peanuts - crushed on a chakla-belan or ground to a coarse powder in a small spice grinder
3-4 drops kewra essence, 4 tbsp cornflour
FILLING
2 onions - sliced and deep fried till golden brown
5-6 tbsp very finely chopped poodina (mint)
2-3 drops of kewra essence
1 tbsp kishmish - soaked in water
4 tbsp thick malai, ¼ tsp salt

1. Pressure cook potatoes, cauliflower, onion and peas with 1 cup water to give one whistle. Keep on low flame for 5 minutes. Remove from fire. Cool. Drain and leave in a sieve(channi) for about 5 minutes to remove excess moisture.

2. Return the vegetables to the cooker. Mash the vegetables with a potato masher and keep on fire for 2 minutes to dry completely. Remove from fire.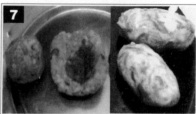

3. Add ginger- garlic, red chilli powder, garam masala, salt and tomato sauce to the mashed vegetables.

4. Roughly tear the poodina leaves into small pieces. (Cutting reduces the fragrance of herbs). Also add green chilli, poodina, peanuts, cornflour and fresh bread crumbs to the mashed vegetables. Add essence and mix again. Keep aside.

5. For filling, mix all ingredients together. Keep aside.

6. Break off balls of the vegetable mixture and pat them into flat oval shapes about ½" thick.

7. Place a row of filling along the length. Pick up the sides to cover the filling and shape into rolls. Deep fry till golden.

Party Snacks -
FROM AROUND THE WORLD

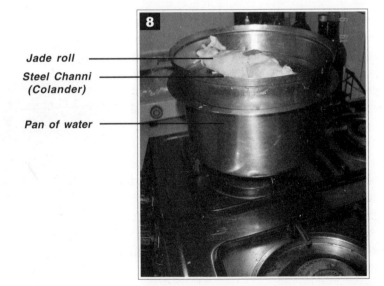

8

Jade roll ————

Steel Channi ————
(Colander)

Pan of water ————

Lotus Wings

Serves 4

200 gm lotus stem (bhein) - peeled & cut diagonally into thin slices
2 spring onions - cut white part into rings and greens into 1" diagonal pieces, (keep greens separate)
1-2 green chillies - chopped finely
4-5 flakes garlic - crushed (optional)
¼ tsp each of ajinomoto, salt, pepper, sugar
1 tbsp soya sauce, 1 tbsp red chilli sauce
1½ tbsp tomato ketchup, ½ tbsp vinegar
1 tbsp honey
1 tbsp coriander - chopped

BATTER
4 tbsp plain flour (maida), 4 tbsp cornflour
2 flakes garlic - crushed to a paste
½ tsp salt, ¼ tsp pepper

1. Cut lotus stem diagonally into thin slices.
2. To parboil lotus stem, boil 4 cups water with 1 tsp salt. Add sliced lotus stem to boiling water. Boil for 2 minutes. Strain. Refresh in cold water. Strain and keep aside. Wipe dry on a clean kitchen towel.

3. Cut white bulb of spring onion into rings and cut green part diagonally into 1" pieces.
4. For batter- mix maida, cornflour, garlic, salt & pepper. Add just enough water, to make a batter of a thick coating consistency, such that it coats the slices.

5. Dip each piece in batter. Deep fry in two batches to a golden yellow colour. Keep aside.
6. Heat 2 tbsp oil in pan. Reduce heat. Fry the green chillies and garlic till garlic just starts to change colour. Add white of spring onions. Add ajinomoto, salt, pepper and sugar.
7. Remove from fire. Add soya sauce, red chilli sauce, tomato ketchup and vinegar. Return to fire. Stir for a few seconds.
8. Add greens of spring onion. Stir for few seconds.
9. Add honey and mix.
10. Add fried lotus stem and coriander. Mix well till dry and the sauce coats the lotus stem. Remove from heat. Serve hot.

Spaghetti & Corn Balls

Serves 4

1 cup boiled spaghetti
½ cup cooked corn kernels (tinned or freshly boiled)
2-3 tbsp grated mozzarella cheese
2 tbsp butter
2½ tbsp maida (plain flour)
4-6 flakes garlic - crushed
1 onion - finely chopped
2 fresh red or green chillies - deseeded and chopped
2 tbsp chopped parsley or coriander
¾ cup milk
½ tsp saboot kali mirch (peppercorns) - crushed, ¾ tsp salt, or to taste

COATING BATTER
¼ cup maida, a little less than ½ cup water
a pinch of salt and pepper

1. Heat butter. Add flour. Stir on low heat for a minute.
2. Add garlic and onion. Cook on low heat for 2 minutes till onions turn soft. Add red or green chillies. Add chopped coriander or parsley.
3. Reduce heat and add milk, stirring continuously. Mix well and cook on medium flame, stirring continuously till thick.
4. Add corn. Mix well. Add salt and pepper to taste.

5. Add boiled spaghetti and cook further till very thick and lumpy.
6. Add cheese. Remove from fire and cool.
7. Make balls with greased hands, only after the mixture turns cold.
8. Heat oil till medium hot.
9. Prepare a thick coating batter with maida and water mixed together. Add a little salt and pepper.
10. Dip each ball in the coating batter and deep fry 3-4 pieces at a time, to a golden brown colour. Serve hot with tomato ketchup.

Honey Potato Fingers

A popular dry dish of saucy and crisp golden potato fingers.

Serves 4

4 large potatoes

BATTER
¼ cup + 2 tbsp flour (maida), ¼ cup cornflour
½ tsp salt, ¼ tsp pepper, a pinch of ajinomoto, ½ tsp soya sauce
2 pinches or drops of orange red colour

OTHER INGREDIENTS
4-5 green chillies - slit lengthwise and deseeded
4-5 flakes garlic - crushed, optional
1 tsp soya sauce
1 tbsp red chilli sauce
2½ tbsp tomato ketchup, ½ tbsp vinegar
2 tsp honey
¼ tsp each of salt and pepper
3 greens of spring onions - cut diagonally into 2" pieces
1 tbsp chopped coriander

1. Peel the potatoes and cut into ¼" thick slices. Cut each slice into ¼" wide fingers. Soak them in salted cold water for 15 minutes. Strain and wipe dry on a clean kitchen towel. Sprinkle 1-2 tbsp cornflour on them to absorb excess water.

2. For batter- mix flour, cornflour, salt, pepper, ajinomoto, soya sauce and colour. Add just enough water, about 3-4 tbsp, to make a batter of a thick pouring consistency, such that it coats the potatoes.

3. Dip fingers of potatoes in the batter and deep fry to a golden orange colour. Check that they get properly cooked on frying. Keep aside, spread out on a plate till the time of serving.

4. At serving time, heat 1 tbsp oil. Reduce heat. Fry the green chillies and garlic till garlic changes colour.

5. Add soya sauce, chilli sauce, tomato ketchup and vinegar. Stir. Add honey.

6. Add salt and pepper. Add 2 tbsp water and greens of spring onions and coriander.

7. Add the fried potatoes. Mix well. Serve hot.

Vegetable Dim Sums

A steamed Chinese snack, something like momos. Use a steamer basket or an idli stand for steaming them.

Makes 14 pieces

DOUGH
1 cup maida, 1 tbsp oil, ¼ tsp salt

FILLING
2 tbsp oil
1 onion - finely chopped
4-5 mushrooms - finely chopped, optional
1 tsp ginger-garlic paste
2 green chillies - finely chopped
1 large carrot - very finely chopped or grated
2 cups very finely chopped cabbage (½ small cabbage)
1 tsp salt & ½ tsp pepper powder, or to taste
1 tsp vinegar

DIPPING SAUCE
4-5 tbsp soya sauce
2 tbsp white vinegar
1-2 tbsp oil
4 flakes garlic - crushed to a paste
½ tsp chilli powder, ¼ tsp salt
2 tsp tomato ketchup

1. For the dough, sift maida with salt. Add oil and knead with enough water to make a stiff dough of rolling consistency, as that for puris.
2. For the filling, heat oil. Add chopped onion. Fry till soft. Add mushrooms and cook further for 2 minutes. Add carrot, green chillies & ginger-garlic paste. Mix well and add the cabbage. Stir fry on high flame for 3 minutes. Add salt, pepper to taste. Add vinegar and mix well. Remove from fire and keep filling aside.
3. Take out the dough and form small balls. Roll out flat, as thin as possible into small rounds of 2½" diameter.
4. Put some stuffing in the centre and make it into a ball. Roll the ball between the hands to give it an elongated shape like a roll.
5. To steam, put them in idlis stands or a steamer and steam for 10 minutes.
6. Cool the dimsums. Cut a slice from the top to expose the filling. Dot with chilli sauce.
7. For dipping sauce, mix all ingredients in a bowl. Serve it with the dipping sauce.

Steamed Jade Rolls

Picture on facing page   *Serves 10*

1 cup maida, 1 tbsp oil, ½ tsp salt, ¼ tsp pepper

FILLING
10-12 spinach leaves
2 tbsp oil, 1 onion - finely chopped, 1 tsp ginger-garlic paste
2 green chillies - finely chopped, 1 large carrot - very finely chopped or grated
2 kheera (cucumbers) - peeled, cut into 4 lengthwise & deseeded (remove seeds)
1 tsp salt & ½ tsp pepper powder, or to taste, 1 tsp vinegar

SAUCE
10-12 flakes garlic & 3-4 dry red chillies deseeded- soak together for 10 minutes and grind to a paste with some water (2 tsp chilli-garlic paste)
**1 tsp soya sauce, 1 tbsp white vinegar, 2 tsp tomato sauce, 1 tsp sugar, ¼ tsp salt,
1½ tsp cornflour mixed with 1 cup water**

1. For the dough, sift maida with salt. Add pepper, oil and knead with enough warm water, to a stiff dough as that for puris. Keep aside covered for 30 minutes.
2. Wash spinach leaves. Discard the stalks. Wrap in a towel and keep aside.
3. For the filling, heat oil. Add onion, green chillies and ginger-garlic paste. Saute for a minute. Add carrots, cucumber, salt, pepper and vinegar. Stir for 2 minutes.
4. Roll out dough on a kitchen platform, into a big, thin rectangle of 8" height x 12" broad. Sprinkle flour on it. Arrange spinach leaves to cover it.
5. Put filling in a row in the center of the strip. The vegetables should be enough to get a heaped row, about 1½" broad, leaving about 3" of maida roti on both sides. (While arranging the filling, the shorter side of roti should face you).
6. Fold bottom to cover filling and then roll the maida covering tightly to get a roll.
7. Seal the edges with maida paste (1tbsp maida mixed with 2 tbsp water).
8. Boil a pan of water. Place a greased steel chhanni (colander) or a steamer basket on it. Place the roll with the joint side down. Steam for 10 minutes (see the picture given below on page 33).
9. Cut into 1" thick rolls with a sharp knife. Keep aside.
10. For the sauce, heat 2 tbsp oil. Remove from fire. Add garlic and chilli paste. Stir for ½ minute. Return to fire. Add soya sauce, vinegar, tomato sauce, sugar and salt. Add cornflour dissolved in water. Give 2-3 quick boils. Remove from fire.
11. At serving time, pour some sauce in a flat serving plate. Arrange rolls on it, pour some sauce on the rolls also and microwave for a minute. Serve.

Note: You may butter the steamed jade roll with softened butter all over after step 8, cut into pieces and grill for 5 minutes at serving time.

Pasta Fritters : Recipe on page 43, Crusty Bread Satay : Recipe on page 57 ➤

Spicy Fried Rice Triangles

Serves 6-8   *Picture on opposite page*

6 PANCAKES
¾ cup maida, 1¼ cups milk
a pinch of baking powder, ½ tsp salt, ¼ tsp pepper

FILLING
¾ cup coriander - finely chopped
2- 3 spring onion greens only - chopped
1½ cups boiled rice - deep fried till crisp golden
4 tsp butter, 2 onions - finely chopped, 2 tsp ginger-garlic paste
2 tsp soya sauce, 2 tsp vinegar, ¼ tsp ajinomoto, 1 tsp salt and ½ tsp pepper

TO ASSEMBLE
2 tsp red chilli sauce
¼ cup maida dissolved in ½ cup water, 4- 5 tbsp oil to fry

1. For the pancakes, mix all ingredients till well blended. Keep aside for 10 minutes. Heat a non stick pan with 1 tsp oil. Remove from fire and pour 1 karchhi full of batter. Rotate the pan gently to spread the batter to a slightly thick pancake of about 5" diameter. Return to fire and cook the pancake till the edges turn light brown. Remove the pancake from the pan, cooking it only on one side. Make 4 such pancakes. Keep on aluminium foil.
2. Boil rice and deep fry till crisp golden. Drain on a paper napkin.
3. Heat butter. Add onions, stir for 2 minutes. Add ginger-garlic paste, soya sauce, vinegar and ajinomoto.
4. Add coriander, greens of spring onions and deep fried rice. Mix well. Add salt and pepper to taste. Remove from fire.
5. Place the pancake on a flat surface, with the brown side up.
6. Spread chilli sauce on half of the pancake. Leave the other side of the pancake without any sauce.
7. Spread 2-3 tbsp of the rice mixture on the chilli sauce side.
8. Pick up the side without the filling and fold to get a semi circle. Press well so that the edges stick together. Keep aside.
9. Mix maida with water in a flat plate.
10. At serving time, heat 4 tbsp oil in a pan. Dip pancake in maida batter on both sides. Shallow fry one pancake at a time carefully till crisp golden on both sides.
11. Cut each fried pancake semicircle into 3 triangular pieces, sprinkle some grated cheese and dot with sauce. Serve hot.

◀ *Tempura (Japanese Fritters) : Recipe on page 53*

Malaysian Spring Rolls

Serves 4-6

WRAPPERS (PANCAKES)
½ cup flour, 1 cup milk
¼ tsp salt, ¼ tsp baking powder
oil for shallow frying

FILLING
5-6 lettuce leaves
½ cup shredded cabbage
½ medium carrot - grated
½ small cucumber - shredded (½ cup)
50 gm piece of bean curd (tofu) or paneer - sauted in a pan till golden and cut into thin long pieces
1½ tbsp oil
4-5 flakes garlic - crushed
2 green chillies - finely chopped, 2 spring onions - shredded
1 tsp soya sauce, ¼ tsp each of salt, pepper and sugar, or to taste

SAUCE
½ tsp garlic paste
1 fresh or dry red chilli - minced or very finely chopped
1 tsp salt, 1 tsp sugar
¼ cup vinegar, ¼ cup water, 1 tsp oil, 1 tsp soya sauce

1. Sift flour and salt. Add milk gradually, beating well to make a smooth thin batter for pancakes. Add baking powder. Mix well.

2. Heat a nonstick pan (not too hot). Remove pan from fire. Pour 1 karchhi (¼ cup) batter on it. Tilt the pan to spread the batter evenly to a medium sized pancake of about 5-6" diameter. Remove when the underside is cooked. Do not cook the other side. Make 4-5 pancakes. Cool the pancakes on aluminium foil.

3. To prepare the sauce, mix all the ingredients together, stirring until sugar dissolves.

4. To prepare filling, heat oil, add garlic. Add chillies and spring onions and cook for 2-3 minutes, stirring occasionally.

5. Add carrot and cabbage. Add bean curd. Add soya sauce, salt, pepper and sugar. Cook for 2-3 minutes. Add cucumber. Mix and remove from fire.

6. Spread a lettuce leaf on each spring roll wrapper and top with 2 tbsp of filling.

7. Fold the right and left side slightly, and holding on, roll upwards to make a parcel. Wet the edges to stick them together.

8. You can serve the spring rolls as it is or pan fried in 2 tbsp oil. Serve with sauce.

Pasta Fritters

Boiled pasta tubes are stuffed and deep fried till golden. The vegetables for the filling should be very finely chopped, so that they can be filled easily in the pasta.

Serves 4   *Picture on page 39*

1 cup uncooked penne pasta - boiled

FILLING
1½ tbsp olive oil or butter, 4 flakes garlic - crushed
7-8 mushrooms - chopped very finely
½ onion - chopped very finely , ½ green capsicum - chopped very finely
½ cup very finely grated cheddar cheese (cubes)
1 tsp oregano or ½ tsp roughly crushed ajwain (carom seeds)
½ tsp salt & ½ tsp freshly ground pepper, or to taste

BATTER
3 tbsp cornflour, 4 tbsp maida, ½ tsp oregano, ¼ tsp salt
2 tbsp finely chopped parsley or coriander, ½- ¾ cup water

1. Boil 8 cups water with 2 tsp salt. Add pasta to the boiling water. Stir well. Boil for about 4- 5 minutes till done. Strain. Add fresh water to refresh the pasta and strain again. Sprinkle 1 tsp oil on the pasta. Keep aside.
2. For the filling- heat butter in a pan or kadhai. Add garlic. Stir for a few seconds.
3. Add mushroom & onions. Cook for 2 minutes on high flame. Remove from fire.
4. Add salt, pepper and capsicum. Mix well. Add very finely grated cheese.
5. Take each piece of boiled pasta and from the holes on the sides, fill the filling with your hands. Start filling from one side, when stuck turn or shift to the other side and fill from there. Fill each piece of pasta, nicely and gently.
6. Mix all ingredients of the batter & keep aside.
7. At serving time, heat oil in a karahi. Dip each stuffed pasta in the batter and deep fry a few pieces of pasta at a time till golden. Serve with mustard sauce.

Note: Buy imported penne pasta for this recipe, as it is bigger in size and can be filled easily.

Pina-Mushroom Crostini

Italian crostinis are small, thick toasts topped with a variety of ingredients and cheese. These make wonderful starters.

Serves 6-8

1 loaf french bread - cut into ½" thick slices
½-¾ cup chopped pineapple
200 gm mushrooms - chopped to get small pieces
2 tsp garlic paste or finely chopped garlic
½ tsp salt, ½ tsp pepper
½ tsp oregano or ¼ tsp ajwain (roughly crushed)
1 big tomato - pureed in the mixer (½ cup)

GARLIC BUTTER
3- 4 tbsp softened butter
4- 5 flakes garlic - crushed
a pinch of salt
¼ tsp freshly crushed peppercorns (saboot kali mirch)
¼ tsp oregano or ¼ tsp crushed ajwain (carom seeds)

TOPPING
some chilli flakes to sprinkle
1 cup grated cheese, preferably parmesan or mozzarella
1 very small yellow or green capsicum- sliced very thinly to get small strips
2 tbsp olive oil or any cooking oil, optional

1. Heat 2 tbsp oil. Reduce heat. Add garlic paste. Cook till it starts to change colour.
2. Add mushrooms and stir fry till dry. Add salt, pepper, oregano and tomato puree.
3. Cook till puree turns dry. Add chopped pineapple. Stir. Remove from fire.
4. Prepare garlic butter by mixing softened butter with garlic, salt, pepper & oregano.
5. Cut French loaf diagonally into ½" thick slices.
6. On each slice spread some garlic butter. Sprinkle some chilli flakes.
7. Spread 1-2 tbsp of the mushroom mixture. Cover with grated cheese. Top with capsicum strips to get a cross. Spoon a little olive oil on top.
8. Bake in a preheated oven at 180°C for 8- 10 minutes or till the base of the bread turns crisp and the cheese melts. Serve hot.

Note: Size of a french loaf is different in every shop. I have given the topping according to a medium sized loaf. If the loaf is bigger in size than the usual loaf, then increase the quantity of the topping. Make the topping 1½ times.

Chilli Vegetable Skewers

Serves 12

150 gms paneer - cut into 1" squares
100 gm baby corns - cut into 2 pieces widthwise
1 large capsicum - cut into ½" pieces
1 tomato - pulp removed and cut into ½" pieces
3 tbsp oil
4-5 flakes garlic - crushed
1 tbsp vinegar, 1½ tbsp soya sauce
3 tbsp tomato ketchup
½ tbsp chilli sauce
½ tsp salt and ½ tsp pepper, or to taste

THICK COATING BATTER
¼ cup maida
½ tsp salt, ¼ pepper, ¼ cup water

1. Cut paneer into 1" squares, capsicum cut into ½" pieces.
2. Cut baby corns widthwise into half to get 2 pieces.
3. Mix all ingredients of the coating batter.
4. Dip the paneer and babycorns in maida batter and deep fry till golden brown. Keep aside.

5. Heat 3 tbsp oil. Reduce heat. Add garlic. Let it turn light brown.
6. Remove from fire. Add vinegar, soya sauce, tomato ketchup, chilli sauce, salt and pepper. Return to fire and cook the sauces on low heat for ½ minute.
7. Add baby corns. Stir for 2-3 minutes.

8. Add capsicum, paneer and tomato pieces. Mix well. Stir for 1-2 minutes. Remove from fire.
9. Thread (pass) a capsicum, then a baby corn, then a paneer and lastly a tomato piece on each tooth pick. Serve.

Leafy Sushi Rolls

A cold snack. A treat on a hot summer day.

Serves 6

½ cup short grained rice (or ordinary permal rice)
a bunch of lettuce leaves - dipped in cold water & refrigerated for 3 hours till crisp

SEASONING FOR RICE
1½ tsp white vinegar, 1 tbsp sugar, ½ tsp salt

FILLING
1 cup finely chopped mushroom
1 big onion - chopped finely, 1 tsp finely chopped garlic
salt & pepper to taste, ¼ tsp soya sauce, ½ tsp vinegar

1. Wash rice several times in water. Drain. Keep in a strainer for ½ hour.
2. Put in a pan with 2½ cups water. Boil. Cover and cook on low heat till water gets absorbed and the rice is soft.
3. Mix seasoning ingredients together. Heat slightly till the sugar gets completely dissolved. Do not boil. Remove from fire. Let it cool down.
4. Spread rice in a tray. Pour the cooled dressing over the rice and mix gently but thoroughly. Let it sit for 15-20 minutes.
5. For the filling, heat 3 tbsp oil. Add garlic, onion and mushrooms. Stir for 2- 3 minutes. Add salt, pepper, soya sauce and vinegar to taste. Mix, remove from fire.
6. Take a 3" rectangular piece of lettuce leaf (trim the stalk side of the leaf to get a rectangular shape). Place the wrong side up on a flat surface.

7. Smear or rub some oil on the leaf.
8. Place 2 tbsp rice on the leaf, leaving the edges. Put a row of vegetable filling on the rice about 1" wide in the centre. Do not cover the rice completely with the filling. Let all four sides of the rice show.

9. Roll the leaf starting from the right side moving towards the left side to get a roll. Keep aside with the joint side down. Insert a toothpick in the centre to secure the roll.
10. Serve cold or at room temperature with sweet chilli dip (see page 92).

Falafel

Falafel are spicy chickpea croquettes (tikkis). These are eaten as a snack.

Makes 14   Picture on backcover

1¼ cups chickpeas (safeed kabuli channas) - soaked overnight with a pinch of mitha soda (soda-bi-carb)
½ tsp hing (asafoetida powder)
1 cup chopped parsley, 1½ tsp salt, ½ tsp freshly ground black pepper corns
½ tsp baking powder, 2 bread slices - crumbled in a mixer to get fresh crumbs
GRIND TO A PASTE
2 tsp saboot dhania (coriander seeds), 2 tsp jeera (cumin seeds), 5-6 flakes garlic

FRYING
4 tbsp maida - to coat, oil for deep frying

1. Soak the channas overnight in water with soda. Drain water.
2. Grind the channas in a blender to a paste. Add all the ingredients except the frying ingredients. Add the dhania-jeera paste also to the ground channas. Mix well, knead and leave aside for ½ hour.
3. Form the mixture into balls. Flatten each ball and then roll in dry maida to coat.
4. Heat oil in a karahi. Dust off the excess maida and deep fry 1-2 falafels at a time, until golden brown. Remove and drain on paper napkins.

Note: For a falafel roll- spread 2 tbsp of hummus dip inside warmed pita bread, put 2 falafel tikkis and serve with hummus dip (given below). Pita bread is available in some good bakery shops. If unavailable, use any regular bread roll.

Hummus Dip

Hummus is a popular Greek dip. Serve it cold with pita or any Eastern bread.

Makes ½ cup   Picture on backcover

1 cup kabuli channa, a pinch of soda, 4 tbsp lemon juice
1 tsp½ tsp hing (asafoetida powder), salt, pepper to taste, 2-3 tbsp olive oil
3 tsp sesame seeds (til), 4-6 flakes garlic

1. Soak the channas overnight with a pinch of soda.
2. Drain the channas. Puree the channas with lemon juice, salt, pepper, 1 tbsp olive oil, hing and minimum amount of water in a liquidizer to get a thick mixture.
3. Roast sesame seeds and garlic on a tawa. Grind sesame seeds and garlic in a spice grinder. Mix sesame paste and 1-2 tbsp olive oil with the channa paste.

Cheesy Nachos

Picture on facing page   *Makes 25*

1 pack ready made nachos or 1 recipe home made nachos (given above)
50-100 gm cheddar cheese - grated (½-1 cup)
1½ tomato - chopped finely, 1 green chilli - deseeded and chopped finely
salt and pepper to taste

1. Make nachos as given above or use 1 ready made nachos packet (about 25 chips).
2. Spread some tomatoes & chillies on each nacho. Sprinkle salt & pepper to taste.
3. Cover with grated cheese on top of each nacho. Repeat on the others.
4. Cover the grill with aluminium foil. Brush it with oil and place the nachos on it.
5. Bake nachos in a pre-heated oven on the prepared wire rack at 180°C/350°F for 5-8 minutes or till cheese melts. Serve with salsa.

Nachos with Salsa

Nachos are fried tortilla chips. They go well with drinks.
They can be made 5-6 days in advance & stored in an airtight container.

Serves 4-5

¾ cup maize flour or corn meal (makai ka atta)
½ cup maida (plain flour), ½ tbsp oil, ¾ tsp salt, ¼ tsp ajwain (carom seeds)
TO SERVE- some readymade salsa

1. Sift both flours and salt together. Add oil and ajwain. Mix well.
2. Knead to a stiff dough (like that for puris) with about ¼ cup warm water. Knead well till smooth and cover and keep aside for 30 minutes.
3. After 30 minutes, knead the dough again.
4. Make small marble sized balls. Roll out into thin chappatis, as thin as you can on a floured board. If the edges break while rolling, do not bother. Roll out thinly into a big round like a chappati. Prick the chappati with a fork all over so that they do not puff on frying.
5. Cut the chappati into 4 pieces to get 4 triangles. Cut each triangle further into 2 pieces to get 8 triangular pieces. Make chips similarly with the left over dough.
6. Deep fry 8-10 pieces on medium flame till they turn golden brown in colour. Do not make them dark in colour. Remove oil by using napkins to absorb excess oil.
7. Fry all chips. Transfer to a clean dry pan. Sprinkle 1 tbsp maida on them. Gently toss to coat maida on the chips to absorb any excess oil. Serve with salsa.

Malai Khumb Tikka : Recipe on page 66 ➢

Mexican Bean Bites

Serves 8   *Picture on opposite page*

1 packet cream cracker biscuits

BEAN TOPPING
¾ cup of readymade baked beans (tin)
1 tbsp butter
1 tbsp chopped coriander or parsley
2 flakes garlic
salt and pepper to taste
a few drops of tabasco

SOUR CREAM
½ cup thick curd - hang for 20 minutes in a muslin cloth
½ tsp salt
¼ tsp freshly crushed pepper
1 green chilli - deseeded and finely chopped

CRUNCHY GARNISH
2-3 tbsp chopped spring onion greens or coriander
2 tbsp roasted peanuts - crushed coarsely

1. To prepare the sour cream, hang curd for 20 minutes. Beat the hung curd till smooth. Add salt and pepper to taste. Mix in very finely chopped green chillies. Keep aside.
2. For the bean topping, heat butter, add garlic and fry till it starts to change colour.
3. Add beans along with the liquid, coriander, pinch of salt and pepper. Cook for 2 minutes. Remove from fire. Add tabasco to taste. Keep aside.
4. At serving time, heat the filling and spread 1¼ tsp of it on each cream cracker, leaving the edges slightly.
5. Pour ¾ tsp (½+¼) of the sour cream in the centre part. Sprinkle some greens of the spring onion. Put a few crushed peanuts. Serve immediately.

Note: Reserve the remaining baked beans in a box for further use. Keep it in the freezer compartment.

Saffron Rice Balls

Makes 12 balls

1 small onion - finely chopped
3 tbsp chopped carrot (cut to get tiny squares)
1½ tbsp butter
½ cup rice (raw)
a few strands of saffron (kesar)
¾ tsp salt, ¾ tsp pepper
¼ tsp red chilli powder
4 tbsp chopped fresh parsley or coriander
1 tbsp finely chopped red or green capsicum
½ cup grated mozzarella cheese
dry bread crumbs to coat

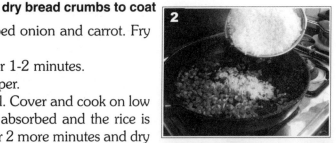

1.   Heat butter. Add chopped onion and carrot. Fry for 1-2 minutes.
2.   Add washed rice. Fry for 1-2 minutes.
3.   Add kesar, salt and pepper.
4.   Add 2½ cups water. Boil. Cover and cook on low heat till all the water is absorbed and the rice is cooked. Cook further for 2 more minutes and dry the rice completely. Remove from fire.
5.   Add parsley/coriander, capsicum and grated cheese. Mix and remove to a shallow bowl. Mix well, mashing the rice lightly so that the mixture starts to bind. Let the mixture cool.

6.   Make balls.
7.   Roll over dry bread crumbs and keep aside in the refrigerator. Do the same with all the rice mixture.
8.   At serving time, deep fry to a golden brown colour. Serve hot with tomato ketchup.

VARIATION
*   Can have plain balls by omitting the saffron.

Tempura (Japanese fritters)

Strips of vegetables, batter fried to get crisp fritters with the colourful vegetable showing nicely. Serve with a thin dipping sauce, but do not soak the tempura for too long in the sauce that it starts to weep!

Serves 4   *Picture on page 40*

4 thick baby corns - cut into 2 lengthwise
1 large capsicum - cut into 8 pieces or squares
¼ of a small cauliflower - cut into flat pieces
1 carrot - cut into 2" long flat slices
2- 3 cabbage leaves- torn to get 2-3 pieces
4 spinach leaves with a little stalk
1 small brinjal - cut into thin flat slices

THIN COATING BATTER
½ cup cornflour
2 tbsp plain flour
1 tsp ginger-garlic paste
½ tsp salt, ¼ tsp white pepper powder
¼ tsp baking powder
1 tsp lemon juice
cold water to make the batter

DIPPING SAUCE
¼ cup vinegar, ¼ cup water
1 tsp oil, 2 tsp soya sauce, 2 tsp tomato sauce
½ tsp garlic paste
1 fresh or dry red chilli - minced or very finely chopped
1 tsp salt, 1 tsp sugar

1. Mix all ingredients of the batter, adding enough cold water (about ¼ to ½ cup) to get a batter of a pouring consistency. Do not make the batter too thick or too thin.
2. Dip the vegetable strips in batter and mix well. The batter should coat the vegetables lightly. If not, sprinkle 2 tbsp more cornflour on the vegetables and mix well.
3. Deep fry 5-6 pieces in hot oil till pale golden (whitish). See that the vegetables show even after frying in batter. Do not make them golden brown. Remove on paper napkin and serve with dipping sauce.
4. To prepare the dipping sauce, mix all ingredients in a bowl. Serve tempuras with dipping sauce.

Baby Corn Cigars
with Tomato Garlic Salsa

Serves 8

200 gm baby corns
2- 3 cloves (laung) - crushed
1 tbsp ginger-garlic paste
1 tsp red chilli paste (soak 8 dry, red chilles in 1 cup warm water for 10 minutes.
Drain and grind to a paste with 3 tbsp water to get 4 tsp paste. Use as required)

BATTER
¼ cup maida (plain flour), ¼ cup besan (gram flour)
¼ tsp baking powder, ¼ tsp salt
3-4 tbsp chopped coriander

TOMATO-GARLIC SALSA
4 large tomatoes - blanched and chopped
2 tbsp vinegar, 3 tbsp tomato ketchup
2-3 tbsp oil
1 tbsp crushed and chopped garlic
3 tsp red chilli paste (use from the remaining paste)
2 tbsp chopped coriander, 1 tsp salt, or to taste

1. Boil 2 cups of water. Add 1 tsp salt and 2-3 crushed laung to it. Add the baby corns and boil for 1-2 minutes. Drain the baby corns. Wipe dry on a clean kitchen towel.
2. Marinate baby corns with ginger-garlic paste and 1 tsp red chilli paste. Sprinkle a pinch of salt also. Mix well. Keep aside till serving time.
3. At serving time, mix all the ingredients of the batter. Add just enough water, about ½ cup, to get a coating consistency.
4. Heat oil in a kadhai. Dip baby corns in the batter and deep fry till golden brown (fry 3-4 pieces at a time). Drain on paper napkins.
5. To prepare the tomato garlic salsa, place the tomatoes in boiling water and boil for 3-4 minutes. Remove and cool slightly. Peel the tomato skin and chop into small pieces.
6. Heat 2-3 tbsp oil. Reduce heat. Add garlic. Stir for few seconds. Add chilli paste and chopped tomatoes. Cook on low heat for 2-3 minutes till sauce turns a little thick. Add vinegar, tomato ketchup, coriander and salt. Remove from heat.
7. To serve, arrange lettuce leaves on a serving plate, place the tomato garlic salsa in the centre and arrange baby corn cigars all around. Serve hot.

Mushroom Hors d'Oeuvres

Sliced garlic bread loaf topped with mushroom topping and grilled in the oven.

Serves 10

1 long garlic bread loaf - cut diagonally into ½" thick slices (10-12 slices)
2 tbsp butter
75 gm pizza cheese (mozzerella) - grated
1 tsp oregano
2 flakes garlic - crushed
8 mushrooms - cut into paper thin slices
1 tbsp chopped fresh basil or parsley
2-3 tbsp olive oil

1. Cut the garlic bread into moderately thick slices diagonally.
2. Mix the butter, cheese, oregano and garlic. Apply this spread lightly on the bread slice.
3. Arrange mushroom slices. Sprinkle chopped green basil or parsley. Drizzle some olive oil with a spoon. Place them on the grill rack.
4. Heat oven to 210°C. Place the grill rack in the centre of the oven and grill the slices (5-7 minutes) till slightly crisp and toasted.
5. To serve, cut each piece into 2 pieces.

Corn & Spinach Balls

Makes 12- 13

1 cup chopped spinach
1 cup tinned or fresh corn kernels
1 tbsp chopped coriander, 1 green chilli - chopped, ½-¾ tsp salt, or to taste
2 tbsp flour (maida), 1 cup milk
2 slices bread- churned in a mixer to get fresh bread crumbs
a few drops of tabasco sauce
3 tbsp butter, oil for frying

1. Heat 3 tbsp butter in a pan, add spinach and cook till soft.
2. Add corn, coriander leaves, green chillies and salt. Mix.
3. Add 2 tbsp flour and cook for a minute.
4. Add milk, stirring continuously till the mixture becomes very dry. Remove from fire. Add fresh bread crumbs and tabasco. Mix well. Let it cool. Check salt.
5. Shape the corn mixture in round balls with wet hands. Keep aside.
6. Heat oil and fry till golden. Serve with sweet chilli dip.

Note: If the balls break on frying, then roll in maida and deep fry.

Unfried & Panfried Snacks

Crusty Bread Satay

Stacks of flavour for a starter - slices of oven-toasted bread, mozzarella cheese, tomatoes and basil or mint with an oil dressing and threaded on a toothpick.

Serves 8   *Picture on page 39*

2 slices bread
100 gm mozzarella cheese - cut into ¼" thick slices & each slice cut into 1" squares
2 tomatoes - each cut into 8 pieces and deseeded
a few fresh basil (tulsi) or mint leaves - place in abowl filled with chilled water and keep in the fridge for 1 hour or more to, make them crisp
a few toothpicks
1- 2 tbsp olive oil
2 tbsp very finely chopped fresh parsley or mint (poodina)

DRESSING (MIX TOGETHER)
2 tbsp vinegar, preferably balsamic vinegar
juice of ½ lemon (1 tbsp), 4 tbsp olive oil
2-3 garlic flakes - crushed to a rough paste
1 tsp dried oregano or ½ tsp roughly crushed ajwain (carom seeds)
¼ tsp each of salt and pepper, or to taste

1. Preheat the oven to 220°C/425°F.
2. Mix all ingredients of the dressing together in a small bowl with an egg beater till well blended. Keep aside.
3. Trim the side crusts from the bread. Brush the slices with the dressing with a brush or a spoon. Cut each slice into 3 strips lengthwise and 3 strips widthwise to get 9 equal squares, about the size of the cheese.
4. Arrange on a baking tray and bake for 3-5 minutes until the squares are pale golden.

5. Remove bread squares from the oven and place them on a board.
6. Spread the cheese squares and tomatoes on a plate. Sprinkle the leftover dressing on them.
7. Push a leaf through the toothpick, then a piece of tomato, then a piece of mozzarella, then another leaf and lastly a piece of bread.
8. Drizzle with some olive oil and sprinkle some salt and pepper if required. Sprinkle chopped parsley. Serve immediately.

Coconut Khandvi

Easy to make, small coconut stuffed rolls made out of gram flour cooked in butter milk.

Serves 6-8

½ cup besan (gram flour)
½ cup curd (not too sour) mixed with 1 cup water to get 1½ cups butter milk
¼ tsp haldi (turmeric powder), ¼ tsp jeera powder (cumin seeds)
½ tsp dhania powder, a pinch of hing (asafoetida) powder, 1 tsp salt

PASTE
½" piece ginger, 1- 2 green chillies

FILLING
1 tbsp oil, ½ tsp rai
1 tbsp grated carrot, 2 tbsp grated fresh coconut, 2 pinches of salt
1 tsp kishmish (raisins)- chopped, 1 tbsp chopped coriander

CHOWNK (TEMPERING)
1½ tbsp oil
½ tsp rai (mustard seeds), 2- 3 green chillies - cut into thin long pieces
a few coriander leaves, 1 tbsp grated fresh coconut - to garnish

1. Mix besan with 1½ cups buttermilk till smooth. Leaving the filling and chownk ingredients, mix all other ingredients as well as the ginger- chilli paste to the besan mixture.
2. Spread a cling film (plastic sheet) on the backside of a big tray. Keep aside.
3. Keep the besan mixture on low heat in a non stick pan. Cook this mixture for about 25 minutes, stirring, till the mixture becomes very thick and translucent. To check if the mixture is done, drop 1 tsp mixture on the tray and spread. Let it cool for a while and check if it comes out easily. If it does, remove mixture from fire, otherwise cook it for another 5 minutes. Remove from fire.
4. While the mixture is still hot, quickly spread some mixture as thinly and evenly as possible on the cling film on the tray. Level it with a knife. Leave aside.
5. For the filling, heat oil. Add rai. After it crackles, add coconut, carrot, kishmish and chopped coriander. Add salt. Mix. Remove from fire.
6. After the besan mixture cools, neaten the 4 border lines with a knife. Cut breadth wise into 2" wide strips. Put 1 tsp filling at one end of each strip. Roll each strip, loosening with a knife initially, to get small cylinders. Arrange in a plate.
7. Prepare the tempering by heating oil in a small pan. Add rai. When rai splutters, add green chillies. Remove from fire and pour the oil on the khandavis arranged in the plate. Garnish with coconut and coriander.

Momos

Delicious Tibetan snacks which are steamed and served with a spicy chutney.

Makes 12

DOUGH
1 cup maida (plain flour), 1 tbsp oil, ¼ tsp salt

FILLING
2 tbsp oil, 1 onion - finely chopped
6 mushrooms - chopped very finely
1 tsp ginger-garlic paste
2 green chillies - finely chopped
1 large carrot - very finely chopped or grated
2½ cups very finely chopped cabbage (1 small cabbage)
1 tsp salt & ½ tsp pepper powder, or to taste
1 tsp vinegar

RED HOT CHUTNEY
2 dry, Kashmiri red chillies - soaked in ¼ cup warm water
6-8 flakes garlic
1 tsp saboot dhania (coriander seeds), 1 tsp jeera (cumin seeds)
1 tbsp oil
½ tsp salt, 1 tsp sugar
3 tbsp vinegar, ½ tsp soya sauce

1. Sift maida with salt. Add oil and knead with enough water to make a stiff dough of rolling consistency, as that for puris.
2. Heat oil. Add chopped onion. Fry till soft. Add mushrooms and cook further for 2 minutes. Add carrot, green chillies and ginger-garlic paste. Mix well and add the cabbage. Stir fry on high flame for 3 minutes. Add salt, pepper and vinegar to taste. Remove from fire and keep filling aside.
3. Make marble sized balls from the dough and roll thinly, to make about 5 inch rounds. Put 1 heaped tbsp of the filling. Pick up the sides into loose folds like frills and keep collecting each fold in the centre, to give a flattened ball (like kachorie) like shape. Make all momos and keep aside.
4. Place the momos in a greased idli stand or steamer and steam it in a pressure cooker with 3 cups water without the whistle for 5-7 minutes.
5. This momo can be had steamed, or it can be baked in the oven at 200°C for 5 minutes till light golden on the edges or fried. Serve with chutney given below.
6. For the chutney, grind the soaked red chillies with 2-3 tbsp water, garlic, dhania, jeera, oil, salt, sugar, soya sauce and vinegar to a paste.

Instant Khaman Dhokla

This light Gujarati snack is quick to make in a microwave.

Yellow dhokla prepared instantly from besan, eno fruit salt and soda bi-carb.

Picture on page 2   *Serves 6*

1½ cups besan (gram flour)
1 cup water, 1 tbsp oil
½ tsp haldi (turmeric)
1 tsp green chilli paste, 1 tsp ginger paste
1 tsp salt, 1 tsp sugar
¼ tsp soda-bi-carb (mitha soda)
1½ tsp eno fruit salt, 2 tsp lemon juice

TEMPERING
2 tbsp oil, 1 tsp rai (mustard seeds)
2-3 green chillies - slit into long pieces
¼ cup white vinegar
¾ cup water, 1 tbsp sugar

1. Grease a 7" diameter round, flat dish with oil. Keep aside.
2. Sift besan through sieve to make it light and free of any lumps.
3. Mix besan, water, oil, turmeric powder, salt, sugar, chilli paste, ginger paste and water to a smooth batter.
4. Add eno fruit salt and soda-bi-carb to the batter and pour lemon juice over it. Beat well for a few seconds.
5. Immediately pour this mixture in the greased dish. Steam for 12- 13 minutes on medium heat, till the back of a spoon inserted in the dhokla comes out clean. OR Microwave uncovered for 6 minutes. Remove from oven and keep aside.
6. To temper, microwave oil, green chillies, rai, water, sugar and vinegar for 4½ minutes. Pour over the dhokla and wait for ½ hour to absorb it and to turn soft.
7. Cool and cut into 1½" pieces.
8. Sprinkle chopped coriander. Serve.

Mushroom Crackers

Cream crackers (savoury biscuits) with a mushroom topping.

Serves 8

16 cream cracker biscuits
75 gms mushrooms - chopped finely (¾ cup)
1 tiny onion - chopped finely
½ capsicum - cut into fine rings, ½ capsicum - chopped finely
3 tbsp butter
2 tbsp maida (plain flour), 1 cup milk
salt to taste, 6-8 saboot kali mirch (peppercorns) - crushed roughly (¼ tsp)
1 green chilli – deseeded and finely chopped
1 small tomato - cut into half and then into slices

1. Heat butter. Add onion and mushrooms. Cook for 2-3 minutes. Add capsicum.
2. Sprinkle maida. Cook for 1-2 minutes on low heat. Remove from fire.
3. Add milk, stirring continuously. Cook on fire until quite thick. Remove from fire. Add salt, freshly crushed pepper and green chillies.
4. Apply this mixture on each biscuit. Garnish with ½ tomato slice and place a halved capsicum ring around the tomato. Serve at room temperature or warm in an oven or microwave 8 pieces together for 1 minute.

Fruity Canapes

Makes 10-12

5-6 slices bread
1 small cucumber - cut into thin slices without peeling and dipped for 30 minutes in
½ cup vinegar to which 1 tsp sugar and 1 tsp salt has been mixed
1 orange, a few fresh or tinned cherry
cheese spread, some bhuna jeera or crushed black pepper
some chaat masala

1. Toast bread slices till crisp. With a cutter or a sharp lid, cut out small rounds (about 1½" diameter) of the each bread or cut sides and then into 2 rectangles.
2. Spread some cheese spread. Sprinkle some bhuna jeera or pepper.
3. Place a pickled cucumber slice. Open an orange segment, cut into half and place it on the side of kheera and top with a cherry.
4. Sprinkle some chaat masala and serve.

Vegetarian Seekh

Picture on page 21   *Makes 15*

1 cup saboot masoor ki dal - soaked for 2 hours in some water
1" piece ginger, 8-10 flakes garlic
1 green chilli - chopped, 1 tsp jeera (cumin seeds)
2 laung (cloves) and seeds of 2 chhoti illaichi (green cardamom) - powdered
3 tbsp cornflour
2 tbsp thick curd
1¼ tsp salt or to taste, 1 tsp garam masala
1 tsp red chilli powder, ¼ tsp amchoor
½ piece of a bread churned in a mixer to get fresh bread crumbs
2½ tsp lemon juice, 3-4 tbsp oil
3 tbsp capsicum - chopped, 3 tbsp onion- chopped
2 tbsp tomato (without pulp)- finely chopped

1. Soak saboot masoor dal for 2 hours. Strain.
2. Grind dal, ginger, garlic, green chilli and jeera to a thick smooth paste using the minimum amount of water. Keep dal paste aside.

3. Heat 3 tbsp oil in a heavy bottomed kadhai. Add dal. Stir-fry for 4-5 minutes on low flame till dal is dry and does not stick to the bottom of the kadhai. Remove.
4. Mix powdered illaichi and laung, cornflour, curd, salt, garam masala, red chilli powder, amchoor and bread crumbs with the dal.

5. Add lemon juice, 2 tbsp of chopped capsicum, 2 tbsp of chopped onion, 1 tbsp of chopped tomato. Reserve the rest. Mix well. Make balls out of the mixture. Keep aside.
6. Take a ball of dal paste & make a 2" long kebab.
7. Take a pencil or a skewer and push it from one end of the kebab to the other without puncturing at any point.
8. Stick remaining chopped onion, capsicum and tomatoes (without pulp) on kebab by pressing vegetables with the palm on to the kebab.
9. Gently pull out the skewer or the pencil.
10. Shallow fry seekh in 4-5 tbsp oil in a pan on medium heat till light brown. Serve hot.

Baked Cabbage Squares

Serves 8

3 cups grated cabbage
1½ cups besan (gram flour)
1½ cups water, 1 tsp very finely chopped ginger
2/3 cup oil
½ cup finely grated fresh coconut or dry coconut powder
2 tbsp fresh coriander, ¼ tsp soda-bi-carb
1 tsp jeera powder, 1 tsp red chilli powder, 1½-2 tsp salt, or to taste
1 tbsp til (white sesame seeds) - for topping

1. Mix all ingredients, except til seeds, together with an egg beater.
2. Put in a greased medium sized, shallow baking dish to get ¾" thick layer (8-9" square dish). Sprinkle some til (sesame seeds) on top.
3. Bake at 180°C/350°F for 60 minutes till it turns brownish. Check with a knife to see if it is done. Leave aside to cool.
4. Cut into 1" squares only after it cools down. Serve at room temperature or warm in a microwave to serve.

Pina-Corn Niblers

Serves 4-5

6 thick baby corns - blanched & cut into half to get 2 smaller pieces
1 tbsp vinegar
1 tbsp olive oil
1 tbsp finely chopped coriander or parsley
3 cubes of cheddar cheese (Britannia) - each cut into 4 pieces
2 rings tinned or fresh pineapple rings - cut into 1" wedges
a few big mint leaves - dipped in ice cold water for 30 minutes
12-15 tinned cherries or fresh grapes
kala namak and bhuna jeera to taste

1. Boil 3 cups water with 1 tsp salt and a pinch of haldi. Add babycorns and boil for 3-4 minutes till soft. Remove from water. Cut into 2 pieces. Wipe dry and put in a bowl. Add ½ tsp salt, vinegar, olive oil and coriander or parsley. Mix well. Keep aside for atleast 10 minutes or more in fridge.
2. Sprinkle kala namak and bhuna jeera on the pineapple.
3. Push through a tooth pick - a cherry, cheese, mint leaf, baby corn, pineapple and end with a mint leaf. Make more sticks. Serve chilled.

Pizza Topped Crackers

Serves 6-8

16 cream crackers
75 gm mozzarella cheese - grated
½ cup tinned corn niblets (green giant)
1 onion - peeled and cut into half and then into semi circles to get strips
1 small capsicum - cut into half and then into semi circles to get strips

SPREAD
1 onion - chopped finely
4-5 flakes garlic - chopped & crushed
2 tomatoes - chopped finely
½ cup ready made tomato puree
1 tbsp tomato sauce
3 tbsp oil

1. To prepare the spread, heat oil in a pan. Add onion and garlic. Saute till onion turns soft and slightly cooked.
2. Add tomatoes. Add salt and pepper. When tomatoes turn soft and well blended, add the puree and tomato ketchup. Cook till thick.
3. Spread 1 tbsp of spread on each cracker.
4. Put some onion and capsicum strips.
5. Pile a tsp of corn niblets and top with grated cheese.
6. Grill in an hot oven till cheese melts for 2-3 minutes or microwave for 1 minute. Serve.

Note: You can store the left over tinned corn in a plastic or steel box in the freezer compartment of the refrigerator for 2 months or even more without getting spoilt.

Kathal Tikka

Serves 6

**300 gms of kathal (jack fruit), a pinch of haldi
2 tbsp oil - to baste (pour on the tikka)**

**MARINADE
1 cup thick curd - hang in a muslin cloth for 30 minutes
1 tbsp tandoori masala
1 tbsp ginger paste
¼ tsp red chilli powder, ¾ tsp salt, 1 tbsp oil
a pinch of tandoori colour or haldi**

**CRUSH TOGETHER TO A ROUGH POWDER
½ tsp bhuna jeera (roasted cumin)
seeds of 2 chhoti illaichi (green cardamom)
3-4 saboot kali mirch (peppercorns)
2-3 blades/pinches of javitri (mace)**

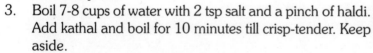

1. Hang curd in a muslin cloth for ½ hour.
2. Rub oil on your hands. Cut the whole big piece of kathal from the middle into two pieces. Remove skin. Cut widthwise from the centre of each piece. This way you get two big strips of kathal. Now further divide each strip into smaller pieces about 1" thickness, carefully to keep the shreds of the piece together. Then further divide into ½" thick pieces.
3. Boil 7-8 cups of water with 2 tsp salt and a pinch of haldi. Add kathal and boil for 10 minutes till crisp-tender. Keep aside.
4. Grind or crush bhuna jeera, seeds of chhoti illaichi, peppercorns and 2-3 pinches of javitri to a rough powder.
5. Mix all the ingredients of the marinade and freshly ground chhoti illaichi-kali mirch powder. Mix in kathal. Let it marinate for an hour in the refrigerator.
6. Place the tikkas on a greased wire rack (jaali). Grill in a gas tandoor or a preheated oven at 180°C for 15 minutes or till the coating gets slightly dry.
7. Spoon some oil or melted butter on it (baste) and grill further for 10 minutes till coating turns absolutely dry. Sprinkle some chaat masala.
8. Serve hot with poodina chutney.

Malai Khumb Tikka

Picture on page 49   *Serves 6-8*

200 gm mushrooms - choose big ones
juice of ½ lemon
1 tbsp butter - melted, for basting (pouring on the tikkas)
chaat masala to sprinkle

MARINADE
2-3 tbsp thick malai or cream
1 cup thick curd - hang in a muslin cloth for 15 minutes
2-4 tbsp grated cheese, preferably mozzarella
2 tbsp oil
1 tbsp cornflour, 1 tbsp ginger paste
¾ tsp salt, 2 tbsp chopped coriander

1. Wash mushrooms well. Trim the end of the stalks neatly.
2. Boil 4-5 cups water with 1 tsp salt and juice of ½ lemon. As soon as the boil comes, add the mushrooms. Let them boil for a minute. Strain and pat dry them on a clean kitchen towel.
3. Squeeze curd and transfer to a bowl. Mix cream, cheese, oil, cornflour, ginger paste, salt and coriander to the hung curd.
4. Marinate the mushrooms in the curd mixture till serving time.
5. To serve, preheat the oven to 180°C. Arrange the marinated mushrooms on a greased wire rack with head side up. Pat the left over marinade on the mushroom heads. You can arrange these on thin skewers also. Grill in a hot oven at 180°C for 15-20 minutes till the coating turns dry.
6. Melt some butter. In between, pour some melted butter on the mushrooms.
7. Remove from oven when the coating turns dry. Sprinkle chaat masala. Serve with mint chutney mixed with a little hung curd. Garnish with onion rings.

Note:

- While threading mushrooms, use thin skewers. Push the skewers gently. They should be woven through the vegetable. This way there are less chances of the food slipping down.
- While skewering or placing pieces of any vegetable, the pieces should be such arranged that there is atleast 1" gap between them so that each piece can get its own space to get cooked.

Mango Chutney Submarine : Recipe on page 82 ➤
Dakshini Squares : Recipe on page 17 ➤

Classic Pizzatini

Serve tiny pizzas with different toppings.

Serves 6

12 ready made cocktail pizza bases
50 gms mozzarella or pizza cheese - grated

TOMATO SPREAD
1 tbsp oil
4-5 flakes of garlic - crushed to a paste (1 tsp)
½ cup ready made tomato puree, 1 tbsp tomato sauce
½ tsp oregano (dried)
¼ tsp salt and 2 pinches pepper, or to taste

ADD ONS
1 tbsp tinned sweet corn kernels or thinly sliced baby corns
1 mushroom - cut into paper thin slices
8-10 spinach leaves, 1 tbsp boiled peas
¼ of a green capsicum - finely chopped (1 tbsp diced)
salt and freshly ground peppercorns and oregano, to taste

1. To prepare the tomato spread, heat 1 tbsp oil. Reduce heat. Add garlic. Stir. Add tomato puree and tomato sauce, salt and pepper. Simmer for 3-4 minutes on low heat. Add oregano. Cook for 2 minutes till thick.

2. Boil 2 cups water with ½ tsp salt. Add spinach. Boil. Remove from fire after 1 minute. Strain and chop. Mix boiled peas with spinach.

3. Spread tomato spread on the pizza bases, leaving the edges clean. Sprinkle some cheese on the tomato spread, reserving some for top.

4. Put corn on 4 bases, mushrooms on the other 4 and blanched spinach and peas on the last 4 bases. Spread capsicum on the mushroom and corn pizzatinis. Sprinkle some salt and pepper. Sprinkle the remaining cheese on all of them. Sprinkle some oregano too on the cheese.

5. Place the pizzas on the wire rack of a hot oven (200°C). Grill for about 8-10 minutes till the base gets crisp and the cheese melts. To get a crisp pizza, oil the bottom of the base a little before grilling.

6. Serve them all together on a platter without cutting, along with some red chilli flakes and mustard sauce.

Note: To make mustard sauce, mix a little cream with some ready-made English mustard paste to get the saucy consistency. To make chilli flakes, coarsely dry-grind the whole red chillies in a small spice grinder.

◁ *Cocktail Corn Fritters : Recipe on page 18*

Raisin Croissant Sandwich

Serves 4

4 croissants
2 tbsp raisins (kishmish) - soaked in water for 10 minutes and strained
4 cheese slices
1 tbsp softened butter or mayonnaise
1 capsicum - cut into half and then cut widthwise into very thin strips
a few cucumber slices - cut paper thin slices
a pinch of salt and ¼ tsp freshly crushed peppercorns
some tomato ketchup and mustard paste to spread

TO TOP
a few olives, some lettuce or cabbage leaves

1. Cut the criossonts into 2 pieces. Spread the top piece with some tomato ketchup.
2. Butter the lower piece of croissant. Press a slice of cheese on it.
3. Place 3-4 paper thin slices of cucumber on cheese slice. Arrange the capsicum strips on it. Sprinkle some raisins, a pinch of salt and pepper. Squeeze some mustard on it.
4. Press the other piece of croissant on top.
5. Tear a small piece of cabbage or lettuce. Pass an olive through a toothpick and pierce the toothpick on the croissants through the leaf. Serve with some potato chips or fingers.

Note: If croissants are not available, use soft dinner rolls or 8 plain slices of bread.

Indian Chana Pizza

There are days when there are leftovers of a meal in the fridge. For e.g. a bowl of chhole, so here is an innovative idea. Ready-made kulchas are topped with home made chhole-bhature's channas and grilled.

Serves 6   *Picture on page 4*

4 ready made kulchas
1½ cups leftover chhole (safed channe)
4 tbsp mango chutney, ready made or home made
1 onion - cut into rings
1 tbsp chopped coriander
1 tsp salt or to taste
½ cup grated paneer
4 tbsp pizza cheese

1. Spread 1 tbsp of mango chutney on a kulcha.
2. Spread some onion rings on it.
3. Heat the channas seperately in a pan with 1 tsp oil. Spread 2- 3 tbsp of hot channas on the mango chutney kulcha.
4. Sprinkle some coriander and salt on it.
5. Sprinkle some grated paneer on it.
6. Bake for about 15 minutes at 180°C or till the kulcha gets crisp. Do not over bake, it turns hard. Cut into pieces and serve hot.

Spread 2- 3 tbsp of hot channas on the kulcha.

Left over channas in a bowl

Quesadillas

Pronounced as 'keseidiyas," LL being pronounced as "Y". A good melting cheese like mozzarella is important for this snack.

Serves 10

FLOUR TORTILLAS
**1½ cups maida (plain flour), ½ cup cornflour, ½ tsp salt
warm water to knead, 4-5 tbsp oil for frying**

FILLING
**150 gm mozzarella cheese - grated (1½ cups)
50 gm processed (cheddar) cheese or paneer - grated (½ cup)
1 green chilli - deseeded and finely chopped
1 tomato - cut into 4 pieces, remove pulp and chop finely
1 onion - very finely chopped
½ cup cooked corn (fresh or tinned)**

SALSA
**5 tomatoes - roasted
1 tbsp oil
2 onions - chopped finely, 2 green chillies - chopped
2 tbsp chopped coriander, 1 tsp vinegar
½ tsp salt, ¼ tsp pepper, or to taste**

1. For the tortillas- sift maida with cornflour and salt. Add warm water very gradually to get a dough. Knead with wet hands till smooth and elastic.
2. Cover with a plastic wrap or a cling film or a damp cloth and keep aside for 15 minutes.
3. Make 7 equal balls. Roll out each ball using a little maida till you get a very thin round of about 8-9" diameter.
4. Heat a tawa (griddle). Cook the tortilla lightly on one side for about a minute and then turn. Reduce heat and cook the other side also for a minute till light brown specs appear. Wrap in a clean napkin and keep aside in a casserole. Make all tortillas similarly. Keep aside.
5. For the filling- mix both the cheese, a pinch of salt and ¼ tsp pepper together in a bowl. Keep cheese aside.
6. In a separate bowl, mix corn, onion, tomato and green chilli. Add ¼ tsp salt and ¼ tsp pepper or to taste. Keep aside till serving time.
7. To prepare the salsa, pierce a tomato with a fork. Hold it over the naked flame to roast it till the skin turns blackish and charred. Roast all the tomatoes like this.

Cool and peel. Chop 2 tomatoes and puree the other 3 tomatoes.

8. Heat oil and saute onion and green chillies till onion turns soft. Add all other ingredients of the salsa and cook for 2-3 minutes. Do not cook further. Remove from fire. Keep aside.

9. At serving time, assemble the quesadillas. Sprinkle 2 tbsp cheese on half of the tortilla. Leave the other half of the tortilla plain, without any cheese.

10. Spread the corn mixture on the cheese spread on half the portion.

11. Sprinkle 2 tbsp cheese again on the corn mixture.

12. Pick up the side without the filling and fold to get a semi circle. Press well so that the edges stick together.

13. For frying filled tortillas- heat 2 tbsp oil in a pan, fry one tortilla at a time carefully till crisp golden on both sides.

14. Cut each fried tortilla semicircle into 3 triangular pieces, sprinkle some grated cheese and dot with sauce. Serve hot with salsa.

Note: Never keep tortilla with a filling for too long, it tends to get soggy. Filled tortilla should be fried as soon as possible.

Broccoli Mayo Wraps

Quick wraps which can be enjoyed as a complete roll for dinner or cut into pieces for tea.

Serves 4

DOUGH
¾ cup maida (plain flour), 1 tbsp oil, ½ tsp salt, a pinch of baking powder

FILLING FOR 4 WRAPS
1 small broccoli- peel & slice the stem and cut florets with long, thin stems
3 tbsp oil
1 tsp finely chopped garlic, 1 tsp jeera (cumin seeds)
1 onion - cut into rings, 1 tomato - chopped
½ tsp dhania powder, ¼ tsp garam masala, ¼ tsp amchoor & ¼ tsp haldi
1 tsp salt, or to taste, 1 tbsp lemon juice

OTHER INGREDIENTS
3- 4 tbsp readymade mayonnaise or mustard sauce, 2 tbsp tomato ketchup

MAIDA PASTE
1 tbsp maida mixed with 2 tbsp water

1. Make a firm dough of flour, oil, baking powder and salt. Keep covered for 20 min.
2. Heat oil for filling. Add jeera and garlic. Wait till it changes colour. Add onion rings and stir till soft. Add broccoli and stir fry for 2-3 minutes. Add dhania powder, garam masala, amchoor and haldi. Add tomato, stir for 2 minutes.
3. Add lemon juice and salt to taste. Remove from fire.
4. Make 4 small balls of the dough. Roll them into thin chappatis with the maida dough, cooking them very lightly on both sides on a tawa (griddle) on low heat.
5. Spread some mayonnaise on each chappati, covering till the sides.
6. To serve, spread some vegetable mixture on the roti. Roll up the roti tightly. Seal the ends with some tomato ketchup (see picture given below).
7. To serve, heat 1 tbsp oil and panfry the wrap with the tucked side down till golden on both sides.

Add broccoli and stir fry for few minutes.

Club Sandwich

A three layered toasted sandwich.

Serves 2-3 *Picture on page 93*

4 tbsp readymade mayonnaise
¼ cup finely chopped capsicum
¼ cup finely shredded cabbage, ¼ cup grated carrot
50 gms paneer- cut into thin slices
¼ tsp pepper, ½ tsp mustard paste
1 cheese slice
1 small cucumber - wash and slice along with the peel into paper thin slices
6 slices white or brown bread, some butter - enough to spread

1. Mix mayonnaise, capsicum, cabbage, carrot, pepper and mustard paste in a bowl. Mix well. Check seasonings. Add more if required.
2. Slice paneer into thin slices and sprinkle salt and pepper on it.
3. Toast all the bread slices and spread some butter on one side of each bread. Place a cheese slice. Lay some cucumber slices on the cheese. Place another buttered toast on it, with the butter side down on the cucumber pieces.
4. Place paneer slice on the bread. Spread some mayonnaise mixture on the last slice of bread and press on the paneer slice. Keep this sandwich aside.
5. Repeat with the other slices to make another sandwich.
6. Trim the edges of a sandwich and cut each sandwich diagonally into four pieces. Serve sandwich with french fries and tomato ketchup.
7. To decorate the sandwich, pierce a small piece of lettuce or cabbage leaf through a tooth pick and top with a cherry or grape or an olive.

Variation: You can also use a thin vegetable cutlet instead of the paneer slice.

Lemoni Seviyaan

Serves 4

2 cups (200 gm) seviyaan (Bambino vermicelli)
2 tsp salt, 1 tsp oil
3 tbsp oil
1 tbsp channa dal, 1 tbsp urad dal
1 tsp jeera (cumin seeds)
1 tsp sarson (mustard seeds)
a few curry leaves, 2-3 dry red chillies - broken into pieces
1 onion - chopped
¼ tsp haldi
juice of 1 large lemon, 1¼ tsp salt, or to taste, ¼ cup chopped coriander

CRISPY CURRY PATTAS (CURRY LEAVES)
1 tbsp oil
¼ cup curry leaves (5-6 sprigs) - washed and pat dried on a clean kitchen towel

1. Boil 8 cups of water with 2 tsp salt and 1 tsp oil. Add seviyaan and cook just for a few minutes till tender. Refresh in cold water several times (like the way you do for noodles). Strain and keep aside in the strainer.
2. Heat oil in a kadhai. Reduce heat. Add both dals. Stir on low heat till they slightly change colour.
3. Add the jeera and sarson and stir to mix. Wait till jeera turns golden.
4. Add curry leaves and red chillies.
5. Add chopped onion and cook on low heat till it turns light brown and the dals are also done. If you like the dals soft, cover for a while and cook till dals turn soft.
6. Add haldi and mix well.
7. Add boiled seviyaan. Add lemon juice, salt and coriander leaves. Mix well gently and transfer to a serving dish. Keep aside.
8. Heat 1 tbsp oil in a small kadhai. Add ¼ cup curry leaves (leaves from 5-6 sprigs). Remove from fire. Stir. Wait for a minute till leaves turn crisp. Spoon the crisp leaves on the ready seviyaan in the dish.

Note: If using rice seviyaan, do not boil them. Simply soak them in hot water for 2-3 minutes till soft. Then refresh in cold water.

Sliced Potato Toasts

Serves 8 toasts

100 gms mozzarella cheese, 100 gms cheddar cheese
1 small cabbage, 3-4 firm tomatoes - cut into slices
2 big boiled potatoes, 250 gms paneer
salt, pepper to taste, 3-4 tbsp butter, 8 bread slices

1. Cut paneer and potatoes into thin slices.
2. Heat 2 tbsp butter in a nonstick pan. Put a slice of potato on it and then shift to the side. Turn when the under side is light brown.
3. Repeat with the other potato slices. Let them be on the sides of the pan.
4. Put some more butter. Saute the paneer slightly. Shift to the sides.
5. Place the cabbage leaves also on the hot pan. Remove from heat. Leave everything in the pan.
6. Lightly toast the bread slices. Remove crust. Butter them.
7. On each toast spread a cabbage leaf.
8. Cover the leaf with 2 potato slices. Sprinkle salt and pepper.
9. Put paneer slices over the potatoes.
10. Put tomato slices over the paneer.
11. Grate cheese to cover the tomatoes almost completely.
12. Grill in a preheated oven for about 5 minutes till the cheese melts and gets browned a little. Serve immediately surrounded by a few cabbage leaves made crisp by dipping in chilled water for half an hour.

Oat Fudge Fingers

Makes about 6- 7 fingers   *Picture on page 22*

¾ cup oats, ¼ cup sesame seeds (til)
¾ cup brown sugar, 2 tbsp raisins (kishmish)
¾ cup desiccated coconut (coconut powder), ½ cup melted butter

1. Melt butter and sugar in a pan. Stir for 1 minute on low heat. Remove from fire.
2. Add oats, sesame seeds, raisins and coconut. Mix well.
3. Take a small rectangle dish, tin or an aluminium ice tray and place a sheet of aluminium foil on it. Grease the foil with oil. Now spread the mixture on it in such a way to get an ½" thick layer.
4. Bake in a preheated oven at 150°C for about 10-12 minutes till light golden. Remove from oven.
5. Let it come to room temperature and cut immediately into fingers, otherwise it get's hard and is diffcult to cut.

Note: You can use cornflakes instead of oats.

Vegetable Rawa Utthapam

Tiny pancakes sprinkled with sesame seeds to give them a nutty taste.

Serves 4-5

½ cup thick rawa suji (coarse semolina)
¼ tsp baking powder
¼-½ tsp salt or to taste
½ cup curd (approx.)
1 tbsp oil - to sprinkle

TOPPING (MIX TOGETHER)
1 small onion - very finely chopped
1 small capsicum - very finely chopped
1 carrot - grated finely
½ tomato - pulp removed and finely chopped
½ tsp salt
1 tbsp til (sesame seeds)

1. Mix suji with curd to get a thick batter of a soft dropping consistency.
2. Add baking powder and salt and beat well. Keep aside for 10 minutes.
3. Add 2 tbsp water if the batter is too thick.
4. Mix all the ingredients of the topping together in a bowl and keep aside.
5. Heat a non stick tawa on low flame. Sprinkle a little oil on the tawa. Wipe it clean with a napkin.
6. Keeping the flame low, drop ¾ tbsp of batter on the tawa to make a tiny utthapam of 1"-1½" diameter. It should not be too thin, keep it a little thick like an utthapum.
7. Drop more tbsp of batter on the tawa, keeping space between them.
8. When bubbles arise on the utthapams and the sides cook a little, sprinkle some topping mixture on all the utthapams. Press gently with the back of a spoon.
9. Put 1-2 drops of oil on each pancake.
10. Carefully over turn the utthapams to cook the other side. Press gently.
11. Cook on very low heat to cook the pancakes properly.
12. Remove the utthapam on to a plate after 3-4 minutes.
13. Serve hot for breakfast, as an evening snack or as an appetizer.

Snacky Dinners

Naaza

A combination of Pizza and Naan! Naan spread with an Indian tomato spread flavoured with kasoori methi, topped with paneer tikkas and mozzarella cheese, finally grilled in the oven.

Serves 4

2 ready made nans
100-150 gms pizza cheese

TOMATO SPREAD
1-2 tbsp oil
4 flakes garlic - crushed
2 small tomatoes - pureed in a mixer
¼ tsp salt, ¼ tsp garam masala, ¼ tsp red chilli powder
2 tbsp tomato sauce
2 tsp kasoori methi (dry fenugreek leaves)

TOPPING
100 gms paneer - cut into ½" squares
2 tsp kasoori methi (dry fenugreek leaves)
½ green and ½ yellow capsicum - cut into ½" squares, or 1 green one
1 tomato - cut into 4 pieces, deseeded and cut into ½" pieces
1½ tbsp oil
½ onion - cut into ½" squares
¼ tsp each - salt, red chilli powder, haldi and garam masala, or to taste
1 tbsp tomato puree
½ tsp ginger-garlic paste

YOGURT CHUTNEY (MIX TOGETHER)
2 tbsp hari chutney, 3 tbsp curd - whipped till smooth
a pinch of kala namak and bhuna jeera

1. For the tomato spread, heat oil. Add garlic and all other ingredients. Cook till thick.
2. For the topping, heat 1½ tbsp oil. Add onion. Saute till golden. Reduce heat. Add ginger-garlic paste, salt, red chilli powder, haldi and garam masala. Mix. Add tomato puree. Mix well. Add capsicums and tomato. Mix.
3. Add paneer and kasoori methi. Mix well and remove from fire.
4. Brush the naan with 1 tsp oil. Spread some tomato spread.
5. Sprinkle some pizza cheese.
6. Spread paneer topping. Sprinkle some cheese again.
7. Bake for about 15 minutes at 200°C till the paneer gets grilled and the edges of the naan turn brown. Do not over grill, it turns hard! Cut into pieces and serve hot with yogurt chutney.

Chilli Paneer Footlongs

The perfect snack for the ever hungry growing children.

Serves 8

1 loaf long French bread or garlic bread, some butter to spread
100 gm pizza cheese - grated
1 spring onion - chopped along with greens or ¼ capsicum and ¼ onion - chopped
2½ tbsp maida (plain flour)
some crushed peppercorns and red chilli flakes

TOMATO SPREAD
6-8 flakes garlic - crushed
¼ tsp red chilli paste or powder
½ cup ready made tomato puree, 2 tbsp tomato sauce
1 tsp oregano (dried) or ½ tsp ajwain (carom seeds)
salt and pepper to taste
1- 2 tbsp oil

CHILLI PANEER
100 gms paneer - cut into ¼" cubes
½ tbsp soya sauce
½ tbsp vinegar
¼ tsp salt and ¼ tsp pepper
½ tsp red chilli paste or red chilli powder
½ tsp garlic paste (3-4 garlic flakes - crushed)

1. Mix paneer with soya sauce, vinegar, salt, pepper, chilli paste and crushed garlic. Keep aside to marinate for 15 minutes.
2. Sprinkle maida on the paneer. Mix gently to coat. Deep fry in 2 batches till golden brown.
3. To prepare the spread, heat oil. Add garlic and cook till light brown. Add all the other ingredients and cook on low flame till thick. Keep aside.
4. To assemble, cut the loaf into two lengthwise. Butter each piece on the cut surface and the sides too.
5. Spread some tomato spread, sprinkle some grated cheese and then arrange the fried chilli paneer. Press.
6. Top with some spring onions or chopped capsicum and onions. Spread some more cheese. Sprinkle some crushed peppercorns and red chilli flakes. Keep aside till serving time.
7. To serve, grill at 180°C for 8-10 minutes or till cheese melts. Cut into 4 pieces and serve.

Mango Chutney Submarine

A summer special footlong.

Picture on page 67   *Serves 4-5*

1 long garlic bread - cut lengthwise to get 2 thin, long pieces
2 tbsp butter - softened
2 tbsp sweet mango chutney (fun food)
1 kheera - cut into round slices without peeling
2 firm tomatoes - cut into round slices
400 gm paneer
a few poodina (mint) leaves to garnish - dipped in chilled water
2 tbsp oil

SPRINKLE ON PANEER
¼ tsp haldi
½ tsp chilli powder
½ tsp salt
1 tsp chaat masala powder

1. Spread butter on the cut surface of both the pieces of garlic bread, as well as a little on the sides.
2. Place the garlic breads in the oven at 200°C on a wire rack for 10-12 minutes till crisp and light brown on the cut surface. Keep aside.
3. Cut paneer into ¼" thick slices and then cut the slices into round pieces with a kulfi mould (saancha) cover or a biscuit cutter. If you wish, you can cut the slice of paneer diagonally to get small triangles.
4. Sprinkle the paneer on both sides with some chilli powder, salt, haldi and chaat masala.
5. At serving time, heat 2 tbsp oil in a non stick pan. Saute paneer pieces on both sides in 2 tbsp oil till slightly toasted to a nice yellowish-brown colour. Keep aside.
6. To assemble the submarine, apply 1 tbsp mango chutney on each garlic bread.
7. Sprinkle some chaat masala on the kheera and tomato pieces. Sprinkle some chat masala on the paneer also.
8. Place a piece of paneer, then kheera, then tomato and keep repeating all three in the same sequence so as to cover the loaf. Keep paneer, kheera and tomato, slightly overlapping. Insert fresh mint leaves in between the vegetables, so that they show. Serve.

Note: Mango chutney is available in bottles in stores.

Classic Vegetarian Pizza

Forget the expensive restaurant pizza and enjoy this home made one! The toppings can be changed according to your liking. Extra cheese may be added for a melting cheesy pizza.

Serves 4-6   *Picture on page 3*

2 ready-made pizza bases
100-150 gms mozzarella or pizza cheese - grated (1-1½ cups)

TOMATO SPREAD
2 tbsp oil
6-8 flakes of garlic - crushed to a paste
¾ cup ready made tomato puree
2 tbsp tomato ketchup
1 tsp oregano (dried), ½ tsp salt and ¼ tsp pepper

CLASSIC TOPPING
½ cup tinned sweet corn kernels or 50 gm baby corns - cut into half lengthwise
3-4 mushrooms - cut into paper thin slices
1 onion - cut into ½ and then into semi circles or half rings
½ red and ½ green capsicum - cut into ½" pieces
a few black or green olives - sliced
1 firm tomato - cut into 4 pieces, desseded and cut into ½" pieces
salt and freshly ground peppercorns to taste

1   To prepare the tomato spread, heat oil. Add garlic. Stir and add tomato puree and tomato sauce, oregano, salt and pepper. Boil. Simmer for 3-4 minutes on low heat. Remove from heat.

2   Spread tomato spread on each pizza base, leaving the edges.

3   Sprinkle more than half of the cheese on both the bases (reserve a little for the top).

4   Spread capsicum and onions. Sprinkle some salt and pepper. Sprinkle mushrooms and corn.

5   Arrange olives and slices of tomato. Sprinkle the remaining cheese. Sprinkle some oregano too.

6   Grease the wire rack of the oven. Put pizza on the wire rack. Place the pizza in the hot oven. Bake at 200°C for 10-12 minutes or till the base gets crisp and the cheese melts. To get a pan crisp pizza, oil the base a little before baking.

7   Serve hot with chilli flakes and mustard sauce.

Pasta in Tomato Sauce

Serves 4

3 cup unboiled penne or any other shape pasta - boiled
2 medium capsicums - sliced into thin long fingers
2 medium tomatoes - each cut into four pieces, pulp removed and then cut into thin
long pieces
4 tbsp oil, 2 tsp crushed garlic
1 tsp oregano, ¾ tsp pepper, 1½ tsp salt
1 cup readymade tomato puree
1½ cups milk

GARNISH
2 tbsp grated cheese

1. To boil pasta, boil 10 cups water in a large deep pan (patila). Add 2 tsp salt and 1 tbsp oil. Add pasta to boiling water. Stir with a fork. Boil pasta for 7-8 minutes till soft. Do not over cook. Remove from fire and let pasta in hot water for 2 minutes. Strain. Refresh in cold water. Strain.

2. Heat 1 tbsp oil in a kadhai, add ½ tsp garlic, wait for ½ minute. Add boiled pasta, saute for 1-2 minutes. Add ¼ tsp pepper and ½ tsp oregano. Mix, remove pasta from the kadhai.

3. In the same kadhai heat 3 tbsp oil. Add 1½ tsp crushed garlic. Wait till it starts to change colour.

4. Add 1 cup readymade tomato puree. Cook for 3-4 minutes or till oil separates and the puree turns dry.

5. Add ½ tsp pepper, ½ tsp oregano and 1½ tsp salt. Mix. Reduce heat and cook for 1 minute.

6. Add boiled pasta, mix well with spoons. Keep aside till serving time.

7. At serving time, add capsicum, tomato and milk to the pasta which is not hot anymore (It should cool down to room temperature before you add milk). Mix well. Return to fire. Check salt and pepper. Remove from fire. Serve hot with sprinkled grated cheese.

Spring Dosa

Regular dosa with a different filling. Give it a try, you will forget the potato filling!

Makes 20-25   *Picture on page 94*

2 cups sela or ushna chaawal (boiled rice) of ordinary quality
2 cups permal chaawal (ordinary quality rice)
1 cup dhuli urad dal (dehusked black gram dal)
2 tsp methi dana (fenugreek seeds), 2 tsp salt

FILLING
1 medium cabbage - shredded to get thin long strips, 3-4 carrots - grated
6- 8 flakes of garlic- crushed
2 tbsp roasted peanuts (moongphali)
3 tbsp tomato ketchup, 1½ tsp soya sauce, ½ tsp vinegar
a pinch of ajinomoto, ½ tsp salt and ½ tsp pepper, or to taste

1. Soak both rice, dal and fenugreek seeds together in a pan for only 2-3 hours.
2. Grind together finely to a paste, using some of the water in which it was soaked.
3. Add more water to the paste, if required, to get a paste of medium pouring consistency. Add salt. Mix well.
4. Keep aside for 12 hours or overnight in a warm place, to get fermented. After fermentation, the batter rises a little and smells sour.
5. For filling- heat 2 tbsp oil in a kadhai, add garlic let it change colour. Add cabbage and carrot. Mix well and cook for 1-2 minutes or till just done. Do not over cook the vegetables, let them remain crisp.
6. Add peanuts, tomato ketchup, soya sauce, vinegar, ajinomoto, salt and pepper. Mix well. Remove from fire. Check seasonings and keep aside.
7. Mix the batter nicely with a karchhi, before preparing dosas.
8. Heat a non stick tawa on medium flame. Pour a tsp oil on the tawa and rub the tawa with piece of old cloth or paper napkin.
9. Remove tawa from fire and pour 1 heaped karchhi of batter. Spread quickly.
10. Return to fire. Cook till the dosa get little cooked.
11. Pour 2 tsp of oil upon the dosa and the sides. Cover for 1-2 minutes.
12. After it turns golden brown, gently loosen the sides and bottom.
13. Put 2 tbsp of the filling in the centre & spread a little. Fold over from both sides. Remove from tawa. Cut it from the middle diagonally to get 2 small pieces. Serve hot with coconut chutney and sambar.

Tip: For a party you can cut each dosa into four pieces diagonally like you do for a spring roll and serve it with coconut chutney.

Perfect Vegetable Burger

Makes 6

6 fresh readymade burger buns
a few lettuce or cabbage leaves - hard stem removed & torn roughly into two
6 chesse slices (optional)
a few slices of tomatoes (slice 1 medium tomato into 6 slices)
6 tbsp ready made mayonnaise

BURGER (TIKKI)
4 big potatoes - boiled & grated
1 tbsp butter, 1 onion - finely chopped, 2 small carrots - chopped
10-12 french beans - cut into small cubes
2 bread slices - torn into pieces and churned in a mixer to get fresh bread crumbs
1 tsp salt or to taste, ½ tsp chilli powder, 1 tsp oregano, 1 tsp pepper
1½ cup cornflakes - crushed to a rough powder or dry bread crumbs

1. Heat 1 tbsp butter in a kadhai. Add chopped onion and fry till transparent. Add carrots and beans. Cook for 6-7 minutes. Add salt, chilli powder, oregano and pepper. Cook for 2-3 minutes. Mix boiled and grated potatoes. Cook for 5 minuts. Remove burger mixture from fire.

2. Add fresh bread crumbs prepared by churning bread in the mixer to the burger mixture. Check seasonings. Make balls and shape into tikkis (burgers). Keep in the fridge till the time of serving.

3. Crush cornflakes roughly on a chakla belan or in a grinder. Do not make into a very fine powder form. Spread the crushed cornflakes in a plate.

4. Sprinkle some water on the tikkis and immediately roll the moist tikki on the crushed cornflakes or dry bread crumbs. Shallow fry in 2-3 tbsp oil in a non stick pan, till brown and crisp and both sides.

5. To assemble, cut buns into half. Melt 1 tbsp butter in a non stick pan or tawa, saute both pieces in it till crisp. If you wish to avoid the butter, just press the buns on a hot tawa or pan without butter. Remove buns from pan.

6. Put 1 cheese slice at the base of the bun. Arrange 1 lettuce or cabbage leaf on it. Put a hot tikki and top with tomato slice. Cover with the other half of the bun. Sprinkle salt and pepper. Lastly, dot with 1 tbsp mayonnaise on the tomato sllice. Fix a tooth pick and serve hot.

Tip: To make the burger look prettier, fix a piece of cherry, carrot or capsicum in the tooth pick before you pierce it into the bun.

Moong Bhari Pani Puri

Delicious golgappas stuffed with sprouted moong & served with poodina pani.

Serves 4

DOUGH FOR THE PURIS
½ cup suji (fine), ½ cup maida (plain flour)

1. Mix maida and suji and knead a stiff dough with about ¼ cup water. Cover dough with wet muslin cloth and keep aside for 2 hours.
2. Take tiny marble sized balls of dough and roll each into thin puris of 1½" diameter. Keep the dough covered. Keep the puris also covered while making them.
3. Heat oil in a kadhai and fry puris immediately. (Puri should not get dry). Fry puris on low heat, turning twice till golden brown. Store puris in an air tight container.

FILLING
1 cup sprouted moong - boiled or steamed
1 large potato - boiled & chopped
some imli (tamarind) chutney, to taste

POODINA PANI
50 gm poodina or mint leaves (2 bunches)
2 tbsp fresh coriander leaves
1 green chilli
juice of one lemon
2 tsp black salt
1½ tsp salt
1 tsp jeera (cumin seeds)
7-8 saboot kali mirch (black peppercorns)
½ tsp saunf (fennel seeds)

1. For the poodina pani, grind all the ingredients together to a fine paste.
2. Add 2 cups of water to this paste and mix well. Chill pani.
3. To serve, make a hole in the centre of a puri, fill some boiled moong and potato.
4. Add a spoonful of tamarind chutney and fill it with poodina pani.

Note: To make puris, you might get tempted to roll out a big round and then cut into smaller rounds with a sharp lid or a biscuit cutter. But this will not work. Although it is going to take longer, each puri has to be rolled individually.

Bread Bhelpuri

Spicy and delicious!

Picture on page 94   *Serves 4*

3 slices bread
1 onion - chopped finely, 2 green chillies - chopped finely
1 tbsp chopped coriander
1 cup (50 gms) namkeen sev (Bikaneri bhujiya)
1 cup fresh annar ke daane (pomegranate seeds) or 1 tomato - chopped finely
2 tbsp khatti mithi chutney (given below), 2 tbsp poodina (mint) ki chutney
chaat masala and salt to taste

QUICK KHATTI MITHI CHUTNEY
(cook all together till thick)
1 tbsp amchoor (dried mango powder), 3 tbsp sugar or shakkar (gur)
½ tsp bhuna jeera (roasted cumin seeds) powder
¼ tsp red chilli powder, ¼ tsp salt, ¼ tsp kala namak, ¼ tsp garam masala
¼ cup water

1. Mix all ingredients of the khatti mithi chutney together in a small heavy bottomed pan. Cook on low flame, till all the ingredients dissolve properly and the chutney reaches the right consistency. Keep aside to cool.
2. Cut bread slices into (¼") tiny square pieces. Deep fry to a golden brown colour in medium hot oil.
3. Mix onion, annar, green chillies and chopped coriander.
4. Sprinkle some chaat masala. Add chutneys to taste. Mix well. Keep aside.
5. Add fried bread cubes and sev in the end just before serving otherwise they can turn soggy.
6. Arrange one or two cabbage leaves in a bowl. Fill with the prepared bhelpuri and sprinkle some more sev and annar on top.
7. Serve immediately, garnished with lemon wedges otherwise it tends to get soggy.

Tandoori Chaat

Serves 4

2 capsicums - deseed & cut into 1½" pieces (preferably 1 green & 1 red capsicum)
2 tomatoes - each cut into 4 pieces and pulp removed
2 small onions - each cut into 4 pieces
4 fresh pineapple slices - each cut into 4 pieces (see note)
200 gm paneer - cut into 1" cubes (8 pieces)
1 tsp salt, or to taste, 1½ tsp chaat masala, 1 tsp garam masala
1 tbsp tandoori masala or barbecue masala
2 tbsp oil, 2 tbsp lemon juice

1. Mix all the vegetables, pineapple and paneer in a bowl.
2. Sprinkle all the masalas, oil and lemon juice on them. Mix well.
3. Grease the grill or wire rack of the oven or tandoor and first place the paneer, pineapple and onions only on the grill rack. Grill for about 15 minutes, till the edges start to change colour.
4. After the paneer is almost done, put the capsicum and tomatoes also on the wire rack with the paneer etc. Grill for 10 minutes.
5. Remove from the oven straight to the serving plate. Sprinkle some more chaat masala and lemon juice, if you like.

Note: If tinned pineapple is being used, grill it in the second batch with capsicum and tomatoes since it is already soft.

Chatpati Aloo Chaat

Serves 4

4-5 boiled potatoes of medium size
1½ cups shelled, boiled peas
1" piece of ginger - chopped finely, 2-3 green chillies - chopped finely
1 tbsp chaat masala, or to taste
juice of ½ lemon, ¼ tsp amchoor, salt to taste, 5-6 tbsp oil

1. Cut boiled potatoes into one inch pieces.
2. Shallow fry the potato pieces on a tawa or frying pan in 5-6 tbsp oil till brown on all sides. Remove the fried potatoes from the pan. Keep aside.
3. Heat 1 tbsp of oil in a frying pan. Reduce heat and add ginger and green chillies. Stir for a few seconds. Add peas. Stir for a minute. Remove from fire.
4. Add potatoes and all the other ingredients. Add chaat masala to taste. Garnish with fresh coriander leaves.

Fruity Paapri

Serves 4-5

**20 pieces of paapri (ready made paapri for chaat) or golgappas
some fine sev (Bikaneri sev)
½ cup anaar ke dane (fresh pomegranate seeds), preferably red kandhari anaar
2 tbsp finely chopped kheera (cucumber)
1- 2 tbsp finely chopped tomato
1 tbsp chopped coriander leaves
1- 2 green chillies - deseeded & chopped
salt to taste and ¼ tsp saboot kaali mirch (peppercorns) - crushed
2 tbsp imli chutney
chaat masala to sprinkle**

1. Mix anaar ke daane, kheera, tomato, green chillies and coriander. Add salt and crushed black peppercorns to taste.
2. At serving time, spoon the anaar chaat over the flat side of the paapri or make a hole in the golgappa and fill some inside.
3. Put ½ tsp of imli chutney and sprinkle some namkeen sev on top. Sprinkle chat masala. Serve.

Bhuttey Wali Paapri

Serves 4-5

**1 cup corn niblets (cooked bhutte ke daane)
some fine sev (Bikaneri sev), 1-2 tbsp finely chopped fresh coriander
24 pieces of paapri (ready made paapri for chaat)
½ tsp mustard seeds (rai)
1 tbsp curry leaves
2 green chillies - deseeded and chopped
4 tbsp imli chutney or 2 tbsp imli paste mixed with 1 tbsp sugar
½ tsp chilli powder & salt to taste
2 tsp oil**

1. Heat oil in a pan. Splutter mustard seeds and add curry leaves and green chillies.
2. Stir and add the corn niblets. Add imli chutney, salt and chilli powder. Cook on medium heat for a minute till chutney coats the corn. Remove from heat.
3. At serving time, spoon the corn chaat over the paapri. Sprinkle some namkeen sev and garnish with green coriander.

Chutneys & Dips - INDIAN & ORIENTAL

Til Chutney

Sesame seeds are very popular in India. It has a distinctive nutty flavour which goes well as a chutney.

Serves 6

2 tbsp til (sesame seeds)
½ cup poodina (mint) leaves, 3 green chillies, 1 large onion, 1 flake garlic
2½ tbsp tamarind (imli) pulp, ¼ tsp salt or to taste

1. Roast til on a tawa (griddle). Keep 1 tbsp til aside.
2. Grind 1 tbsp roasted til with all the other ingredients in a grinder to a semi-liquid paste with little water if required.
3. Add 1 tbsp roasted til kept aside. Mix well. Serve.

Poodina Chutney

Serves 6

½ cup poodina leaves (½ bunch)
1 cup hara dhania (coriander) - chopped along with the stem
2 green chillies - chopped, 1 onion - chopped
1½ tsp amchoor (dried mango powder), 1½ tsp sugar, ½ tsp salt

1. Wash coriander and mint leaves.
2. Grind all ingredients with just enough water to get the right chutney consistency.

Chilli Garlic Relish

Serves 8

4-5 dry red chillies - deseeded and soaked in ¼ cup water
6-8 flakes garlic, 1 tsp saboot dhania, 1 tsp jeera, 1 tbsp oil
½ tsp salt, 1 tsp sugar, 3 tbsp vinegar, ½ tsp soya sauce

1. For the relish, grind the soaked red chillies along with the water, garlic, dhania, jeera, oil, sugar and vinegar to a thick paste. Add soya sauce.

Dahi Poodina Chutney

Serves 6

GRIND TOGETHER
½ cup poodina (mint), ½ cup hara dhania (green coriander)
2 green chillies, ½ onion, 2 flakes garlic

ADD LATER
1½ cups curd - hang for 15 minutes, 1 tsp oil, 1 tsp lemon juice
a pinch of kala namak, ¼ tsp bhuna jeera(roasted cumin), salt to taste

1. Wash coriander and mint leaves.
2. Grind coriander, mint, green chillies, onion & garlic with a little water to a paste.
3. Beat hung curd well till smooth.
4. To the hung curd, add the green paste, oil, kala namak, bhuna jeera, salt and lemon juice to taste. Goes very well with tandoori food & all other Indian snacks.

Instant Khatti Mithi Chutney

1 tbsp amchoor (dried mango powder)
3 tbsp sugar or shakkar (gur)
½ tsp roasted jeera (cumin seeds)
¼ tsp red chilli powder, ¼ tsp salt, ¼ tsp garam masala, ¼ cup water

1. Mix all ingredients together in a small heavy bottomed pan.
2. Cook on low flame, till all the ingredients dissolve properly and the chutney gets the right consistency. Remove from fire.

Sweet Chilli Dip

3 tbsp sugar, ¼ cup water
1 tbsp honey
1 tsp soya sauce
4 tbsp white vinegar
1-2 tbsp oil
6-8 flakes garlic - crushed to a paste (1 tsp)
½ tsp chilli powder, ¼ tsp salt
1-2 fresh or dry red chillies - very finely chopped or shredded

1. Boil sugar and water till sugar dissolves. Add honey and simmer for 1 minute. Add all other ingredients and remove from fire. Serve.

Club Sandwich : Recipe on page 75 ➢

BEST SELLERS BY *Nita Mehta* (Vegetarian)

Vegetarian
PUNJABI

Vegetarian
MUGHLAI

Vegetarian
CHINESE

Great **Indian** Cooking

SUBZIYAAN
Tasty VEGETABLES for EVERYDAY Cooking

Vegetarian
MICROWAVE

Vegetarian
CONTINENTAL

DESSERTS
Including Low calorie desserts

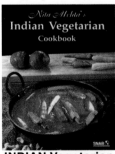

**INDIAN Vegetarian
Cookbook**

**Perfect Vegetarian
Cookery**

Different ways with
PANEER

**Quick
Vegetarian Cooking**

**Vegetarian
Wonders**

INTERNATIONAL
cooking for the Indian kitchen

TANDOORI
Cooking in the OVEN

CONTINENTAL
Vegetarian Cookery

CAKES & CHOCOLATES

Food for Children

Vegetarian CURRIES

Indian LOW FAT

Breakfast Vegetarian

ITALIAN Veg

Green Vegetables

South Indian Favourites

Taste of GUJARAT

Low Calorie Recipes

Indian Vegetarian

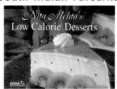
Low Calorie Desserts

Chutneys, Pickles & Squashes

Handi Tawa Kadhai

CHAAWAL

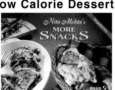
MORE SNACKS

MORE PANEER

JHATPAT KHAANA

Soups Salads Starters

ZERO OIL

Desserts Pudings

LOW FAT Tasty Recipes

ICE-CREAMS

The Art of BAKING

Taste of RAJASTHAN

LOSE WEIGHT

PRESSURE COOKING

MICROWAVE Vegetarian

DINNER MENUS from Around the World

Great Ideas- COOKING TIPS

NITA MEHTA COOKERY CLASSES IN DELHI
At E-159, GK II & 3A/3, Asaf Ali Road (Near C.P.)
CALL TO REGISTER: 29229558, 29218574, 29214011, 9811118056